Res
ear
ch&
Des
ign

Research & Design is dedicated to Bernard and Anne Spitzer
in honor of their generous gift to The City College School of Architecture.
We humbly acknowledge this gift as a vote of confidence in our
school's mission, reflected in the exceptional faculty
work represented here.

Faculty Work

The City College Of New York
Bernard And Anne Spitzer School Of Architecture

Res ear ch& Des ign

OSCAR RIERA OJEDA
PUBLISHERS

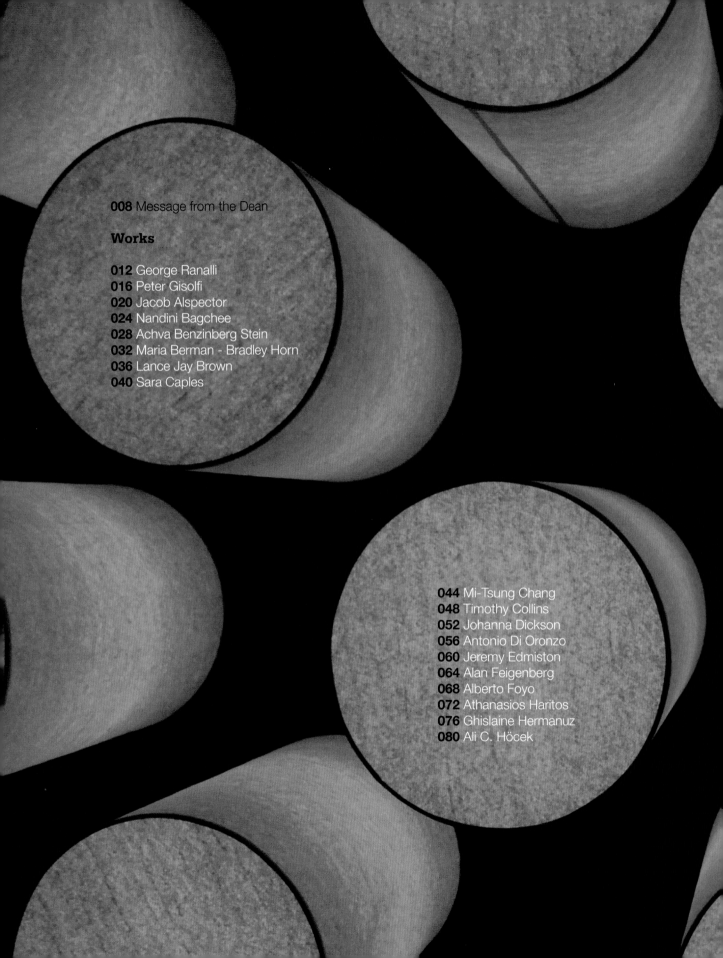

Appendix

Table of Contents

Mes sage from The Dean

The faculty of the Bernard and Anne Spitzer School of Architecture is poised between the theory and practice of architecture. In each case they have dedicated themselves to exploring the prevailing issues in the field in their built and project work while also staying firmly involved in the academic and theoretical realm of the architectural academy. The role of the practitioner/teacher is a model that goes back in history to the first moment architecture moved from the construction site to the school.

Architects who teach utilize the academy as a laboratory for their ideas based on experience first gathered from practice. Specific ideas that appear in some of the built and unbuilt works appear as studio projects where they can be explored more fully, often unencumbered by the practical realities of clients, budgets, and programs. The school is a perfect setting for the architect working in the field who brings professional acumen to the rarified experiments of the academic studio. This book, and accompanying exhibition, are the products of our faculty's professional work: vibrant, intellectually rich, professionally accomplished, and theoretically inclined. The work of the faculty of the Bernard and Anne Spitzer School of Architecture represents the perfect blend of rigorous academic ideas with the practical application of theories placed into the public realm.

George Ranalli
Dean
Bernard and Anne Spitzer School of Architecture
City College of New York
July 2009

Wo
rks

George Ranalli

description The New York City Housing Authority commissioned the renovation of an existing community facility in an 18-story housing block and the addition of a new building. The project converts the existing 1,500 square foot space on the ground floor to a more useable and finished space for recreational programs. The adjoining addition adds a new meeting room, kitchen, bathrooms, and director's office. The addition is connected to the existing building by a long hall perforated with doors and windows for entry and light, and constructed of masonry units that give density and mass to the new structure. All details of the edge of the wall are covered with cast masonry to protect the cavity of the construction.

PHOTOS PAUL WARCHOL

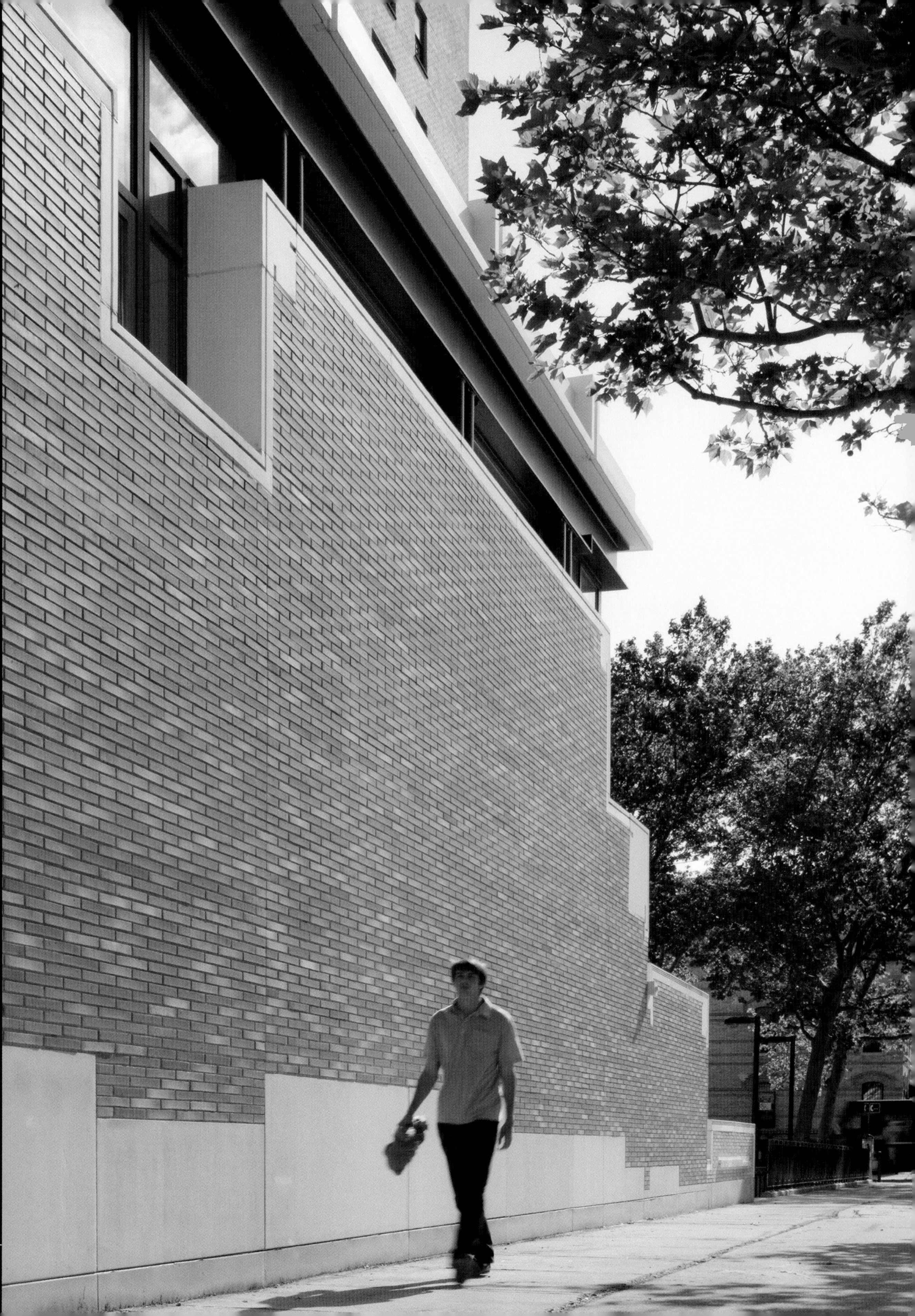

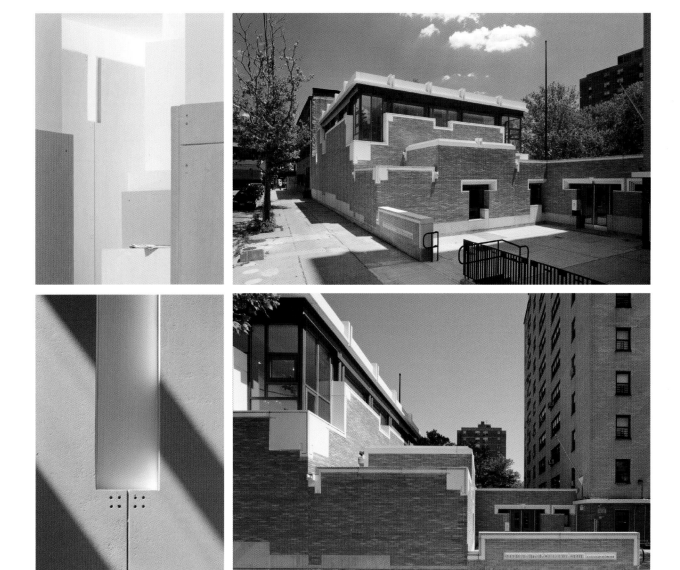

Peter Gisolfi

The Center at Maple Grove, Maple Grove Cemetery, Queens, New York.

description Maple Grove is a non-sectarian cemetery established in 1875 and is listed in the National Register of Historic Places; it is located in Kew Gardens, Queens. • The Center at Maple Grove is an 18,000-square-foot building that will serve the Queens community and will become the new gateway to the 65-acre park-like landscape. The Center answers the needs of present and future generations, serves as a refuge for the spirit, a place of celebration and education, and a space for interment and remembrance. The high wall surrounding the cemetery is opened to the community. A perforated granite wall now extends through the new building and becomes the connecting interior element.

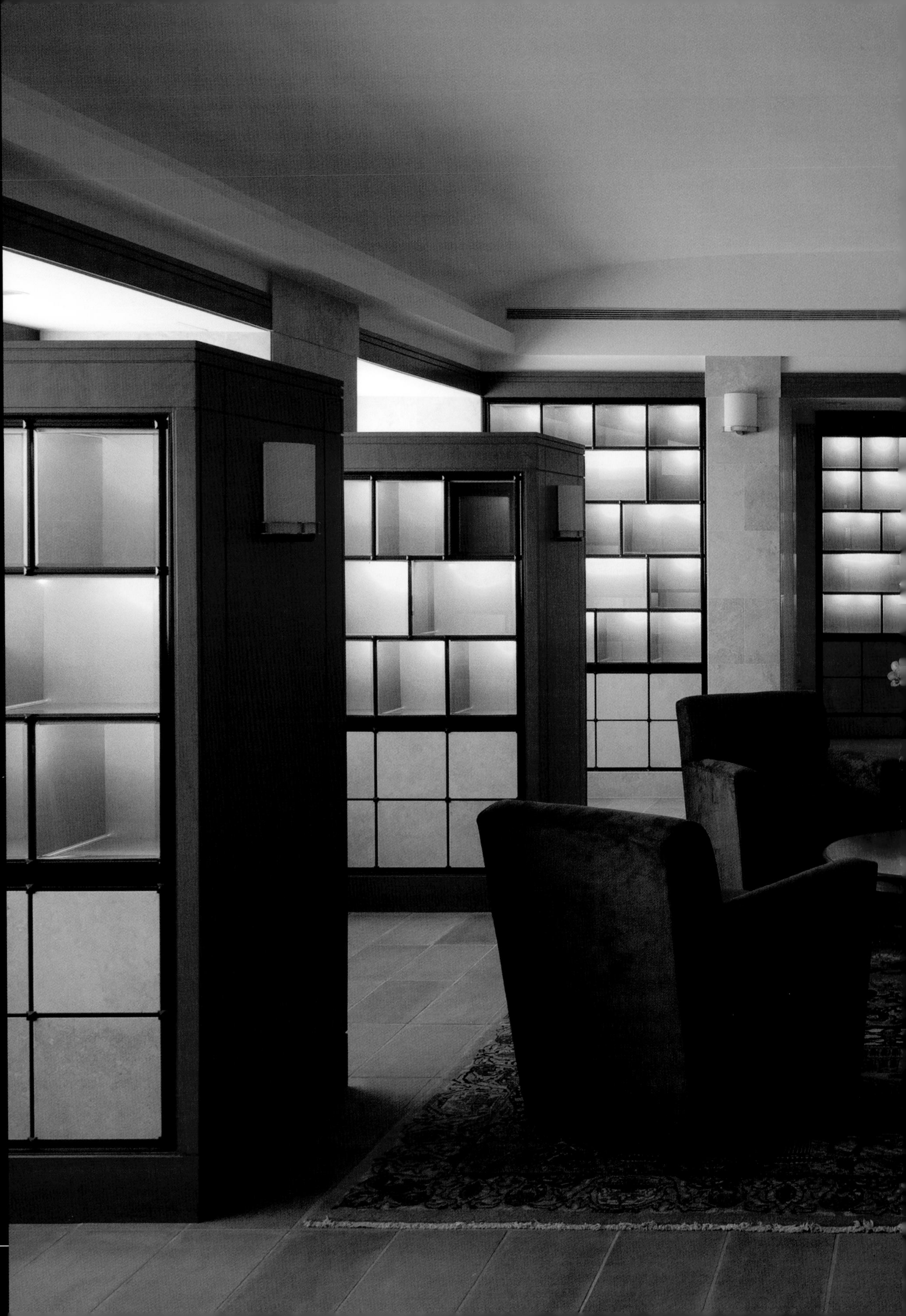

Jacob Alspector

Digital Learning Center,
Utah Valley University
Orem, Utah

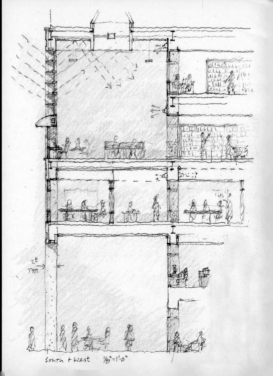

description Utah Valley University's new central library, the Digital Learning Center, completed in 2008, repositions the campus center and redefines the university's architectural and institutional future. Extending and enriching the remarkably consistent modern design vocabulary of the 50 year old campus was an important design goal. An ongoing collaboration with the community produced a resonant, signature building grounded in the college's tradition yet leading the way into the twenty-first century. The first new building defining the future north campus liberal arts quad, the library marks the school's transition from state college to full-fledged university.

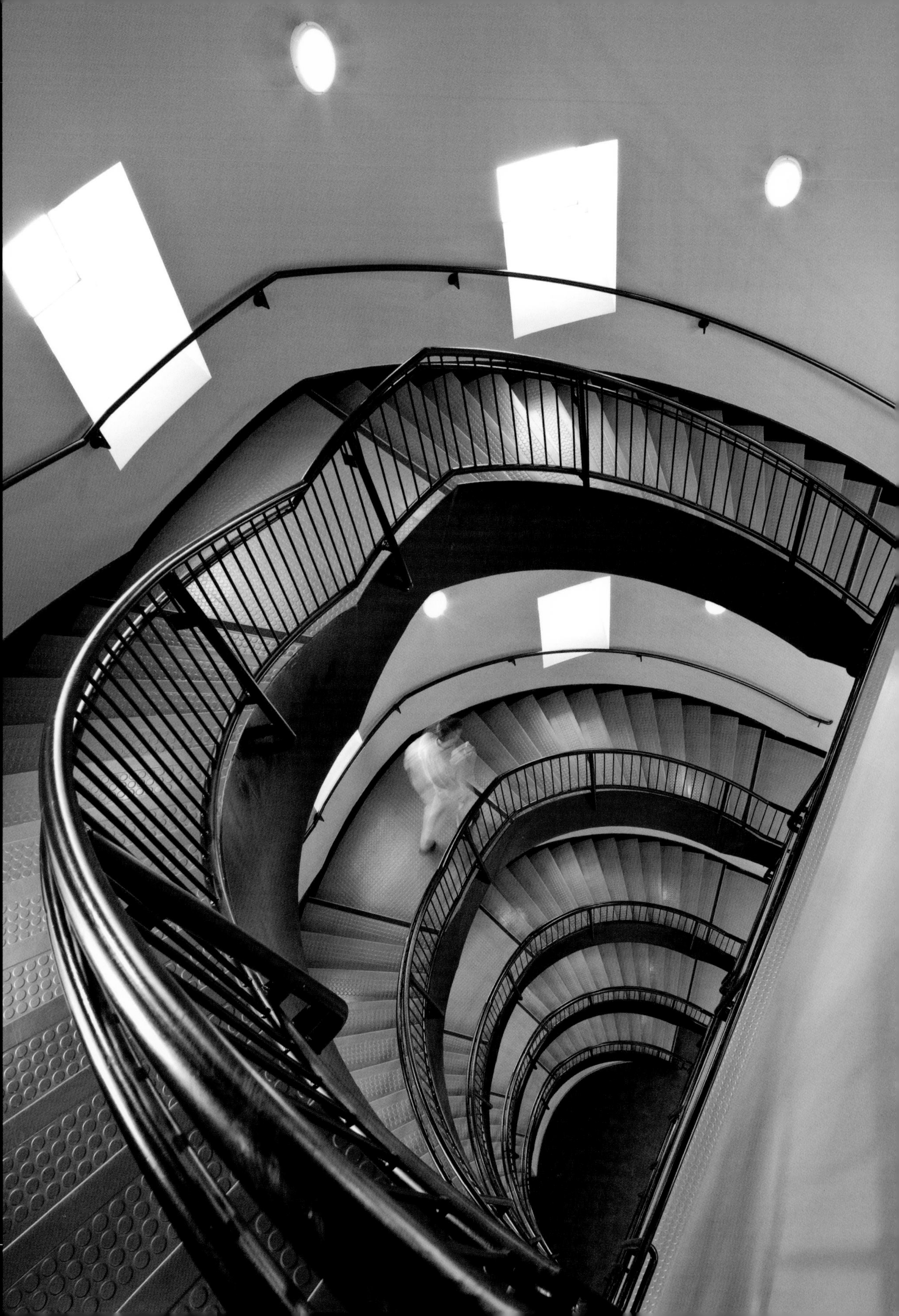

Nandini Bagchee

Stonyhill House, Amagansett, New York
In collaboration with Tim Furzer,
Philip Schmerbeck

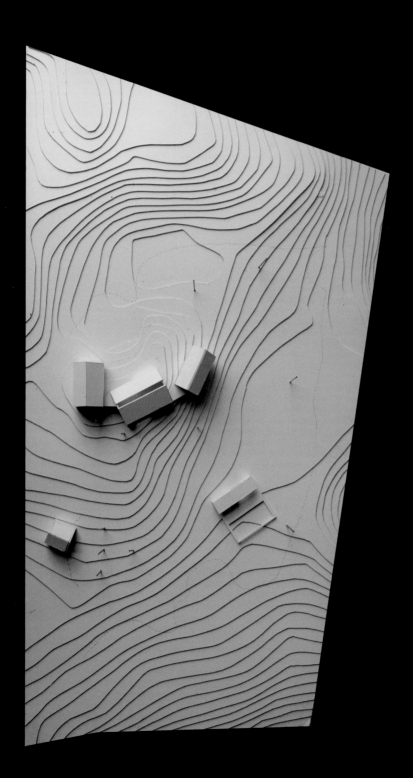

description The house is under construction in close proximity to the sea. A wooded area that opens up to a sloped meadow at the center surrounds the perimeter of the property. The owners intend to use the house as their primary residence and desired a house that opened up to the landscape and took its cues from the vernacular of farmhouses and industrial structures in Long Island. The project was envisioned as a series of five structures scattered on the property and then readjusted in response to views, topography and programmatic constraints. The mass of the main house itself is realized as three volumes: owner's house, guesthouse and a shared "barn" with kitchen, living and dining areas.

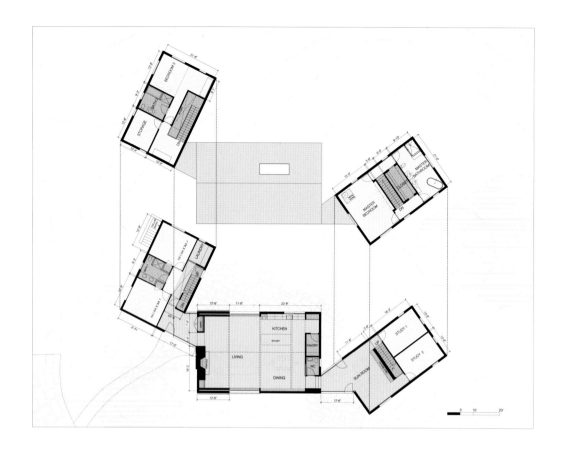

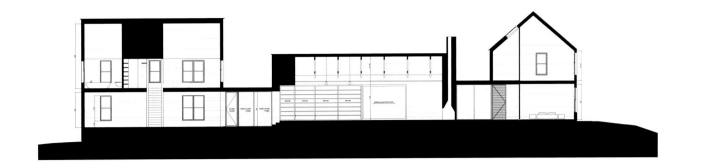

Achva Benzinberg Stein

Manteo
Roanoke Island, NC

description Manteo is the site of the original English colony in the New World. It had gone through difficult times with the decline of the fishing industry but began a revival following the 400th anniversary of its original settlement. As the town recovered and began to grow in the 1990's, however, it also began to attract attention from developers, who threatened to change the character of the town with out of scale shopping centers and oversized housing, violating the well established tradition of modest homes and neighborly relations. A master plan was developed that emphasized appropriate scale and provided day trip attractions for tourists. The plan includes additional affordable housing and a redesign of the main shopping street.

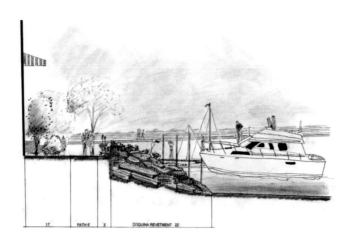

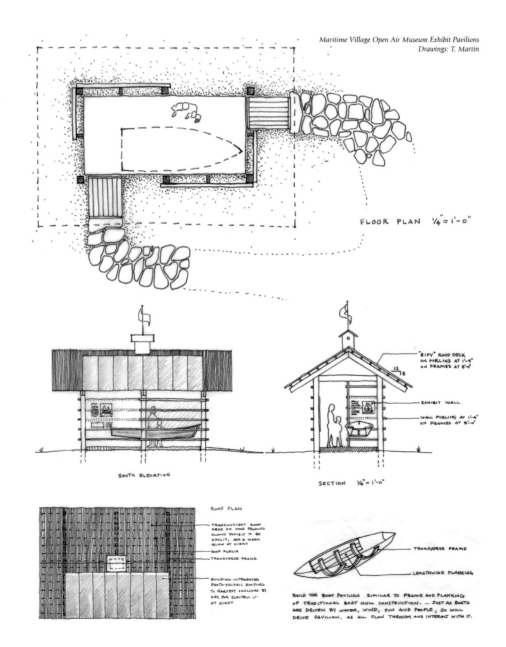

Maritime Village Open Air Museum Exhibit Pavilions
Drawings: T. Martin

FLOOR PLAN ¼"=1'-0"

SOUTH ELEVATION

SECTION ¼"=1'-0"

"BIPV" ROOF DECK
ON PURLINS AT 1'-4"
ON FRAMES AT 8'-0"

EXHIBIT WALL

WALL PURLINS AT 1'-4"
ON FRAMES AT 8'-0"

ROOF PLAN

TRANSLUSCENT ROOF
DECK ON WOOD FRAMING
ALLOWS EXHIBIT TO BE
DAYLIT, AND A WARM
GLOW AT NIGHT

ROOF PURLIN

TRANSVERSE FRAME

BUILDING-INTEGRATED
PHOTO-VOLTAIC ROOFING
TO HARVEST SUNLIGHT BY
DAY FOR ELECTRIC LI
AT NIGHT

TRANSVERSE FRAME

LENGTHWISE PLANKING

BUILD THE BOAT PAVILION SIMILAR TO FRAME AND PLANKING
OF TRADITIONAL BOAT HULL CONSTRUCTION. ... JUST AS BOATS
ARE DRIVEN BY WATER, WIND, SUN AND PEOPLE, SO WILL
DRIVE PAVILION, AS ALL FLOW THROUGH AND INTERACT WITH IT.

Maria Berman
Bradley Horn

Char No. 4
Cobble Hill, Brooklyn,
New York

description Char No. 4 is a southern-inflected restaurant and whiskey bar in a 19th century row house in Brooklyn. The name of the restaurant refers to the practice of burning the inside of oak barrels before the aging process, which gives whiskey its smoky flavor and traditional amber hue. The design takes inspiration from this tradition in its light, color, and in its nod to the form and construction of whiskey barrels both within the pattern of the façade and in custom designed light fixtures. • A field of large cylindrical pendants works tectonically to equalize the difference in height between the front and rear zones of the restaurant, acoustically to baffle sound in the crowded bar area, and atmospherically to suffuse the space with a tawny glow.

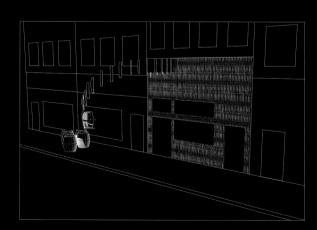

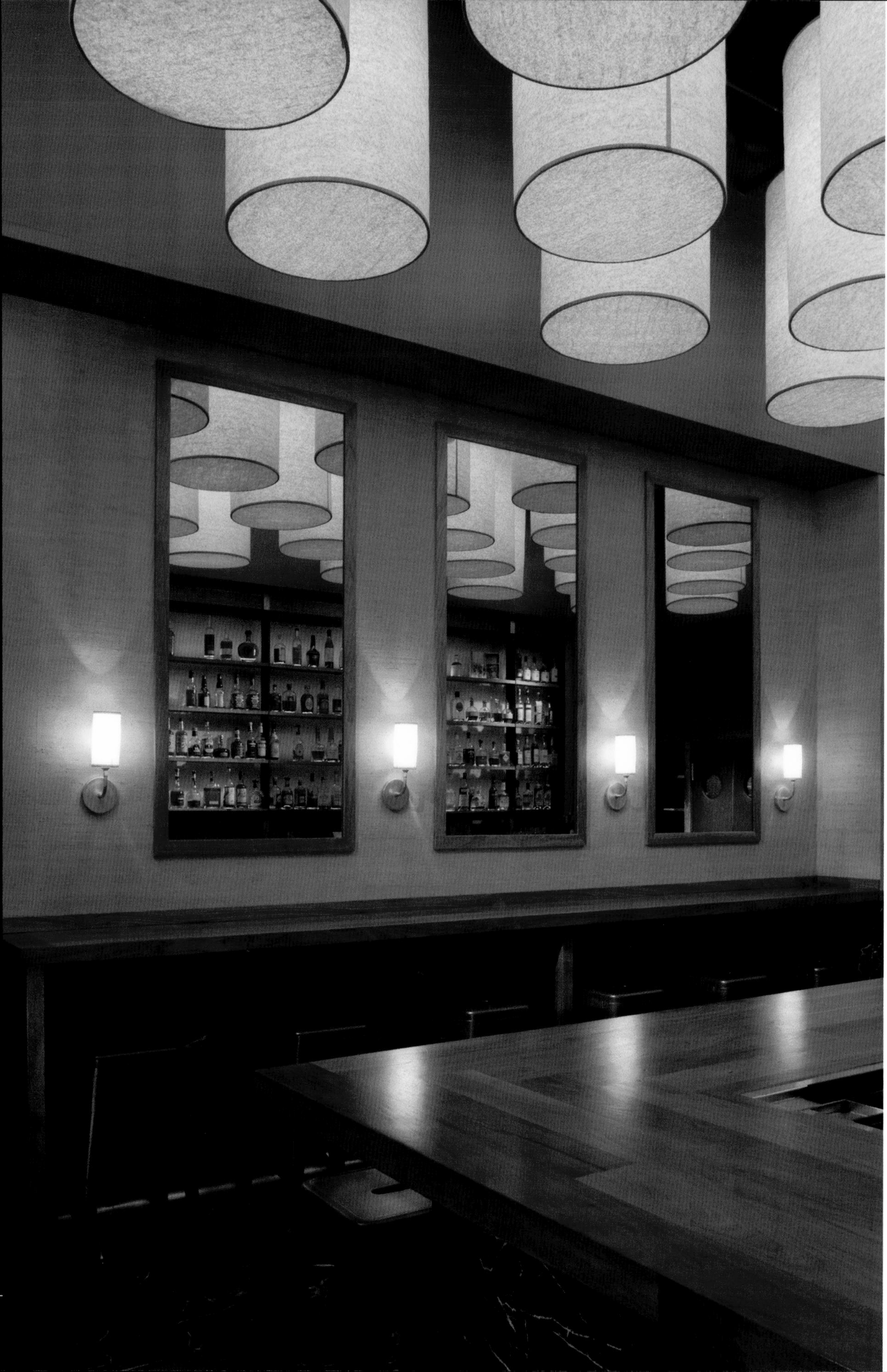

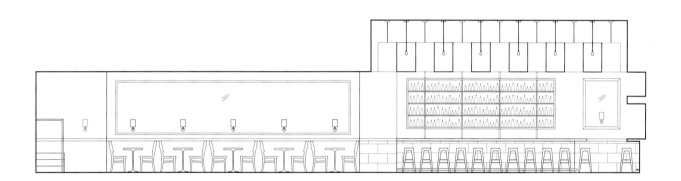

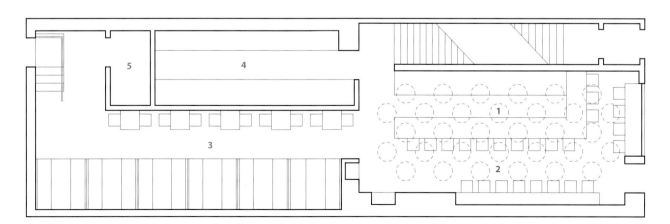

1. Bar
2. Front Seating Area
3. Rear Seating Area
4. Kitchen
5. Bathroom

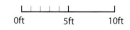

0ft   5ft   10ft

N

Lance Jay Brown

1. Downtown Loft | Architect: 1,500 square foot gut renovation for Planned Parenthood on Eldridge Street on Manhattan's Lower East Side.

2. Urban Design For An Urban Century (Wiley 2009) | Co-author.

3. 9/11 Memorial Competition | Advisor and consultant: Logan Airport 9/11 Memorial International Design Competition.

4. New Housing New York | Founding Member, NHNY Steering Committee: an international competition for the most affordable, greenest, well-designed housing in New York City.

5. Downtown 2020 | Urban Design principal.

6. Un - AIAnyc Annual Conference On Sustainability | Steering Committee Member and Moderator.

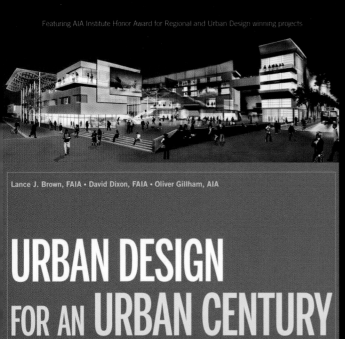

Featuring AIA Institute Honor Award for Regional and Urban Design winning projects

Lance J. Brown, FAIA • David Dixon, FAIA • Oliver Gillham, AIA

URBAN DESIGN
FOR AN URBAN CENTURY
placemaking for people

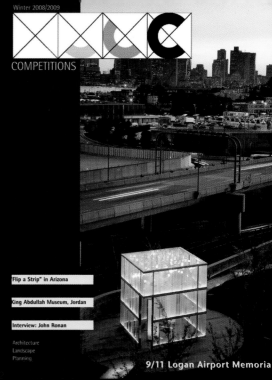

Winter 2008/2009

COMPETITIONS

"Flip a Strip" in Arizona

King Abdullah Museum, Jordan

Interview: John Ronan

Architecture
Landscape
Planning

9/11 Logan Airport Memoria

LEGACY
PROJECT

THE

NEW
HOUSING
NEW YORK

Authors: Lance Jay Brown, FAIA   Mark Ginsberg, FAIA   Tara Siegel

LEGACY

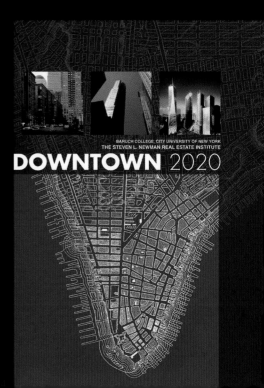

BARUCH COLLEGE, CITY UNIVERSITY OF NEW YORK
THE STEVEN L. NEWMAN REAL ESTATE INSTITUTE

DOWNTOWN 2020

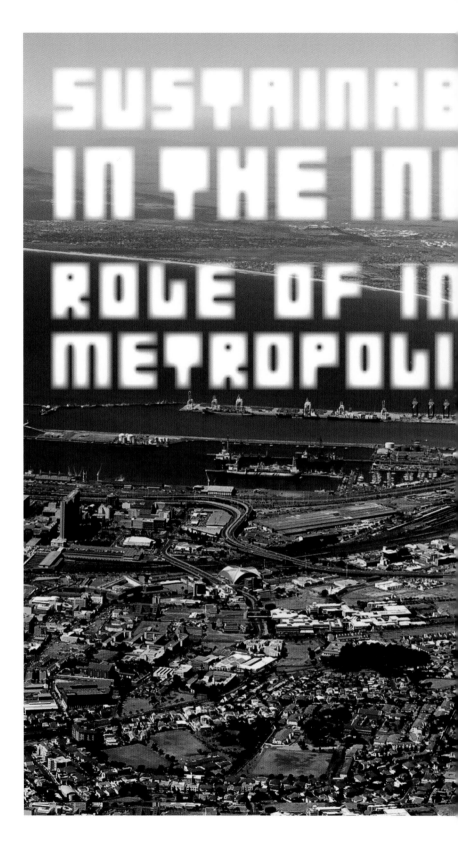

SUSTAINAB
IN THE INN

ROLE OF IN
METROPOLI

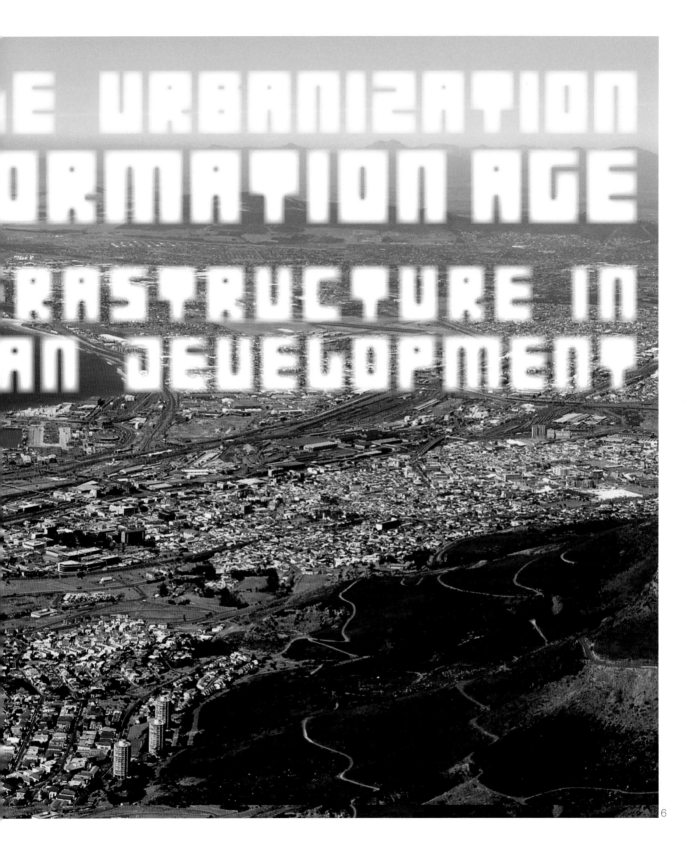

THE URBANIZATION
INFORMATION AGE

INFRASTRUCTURE IN
URBAN DEVELOPMENT

Sara Caples

Marcus Garvey Houses, Brownsville,
Brooklyn, New York
Firm: Caples Jefferson Architects

description The Community Center, an infill in an existing housing development, transforms a former dirt court and dog run into a community asset. The Center's spaces include a multipurpose room for exercise and community gatherings, classrooms for after school and evening programs, a kitchen, offices, and service rooms. Outdoor spaces include a protected inner court for play and meetings, a basketball court, a planted grove, a paved seating area for seniors, a linear playground for toddlers and children, and a shaded walkway for pedestrian and bicycle traffic. Transparent corridors define sheltered spaces at the center of the building while revealing the positive activities within.

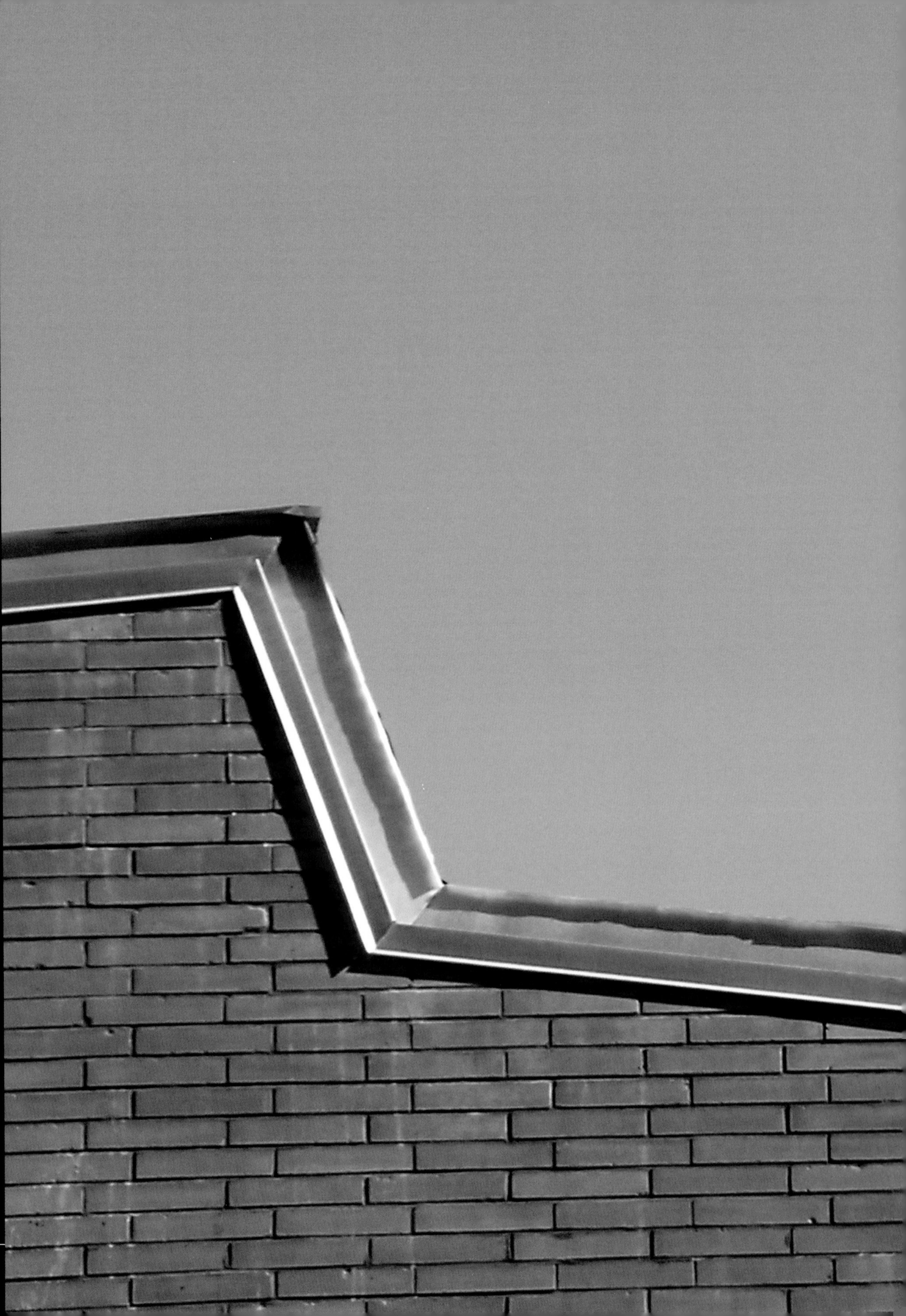

Mi-Tsung Chang

Tunnel Museum of Transit History,
New York City

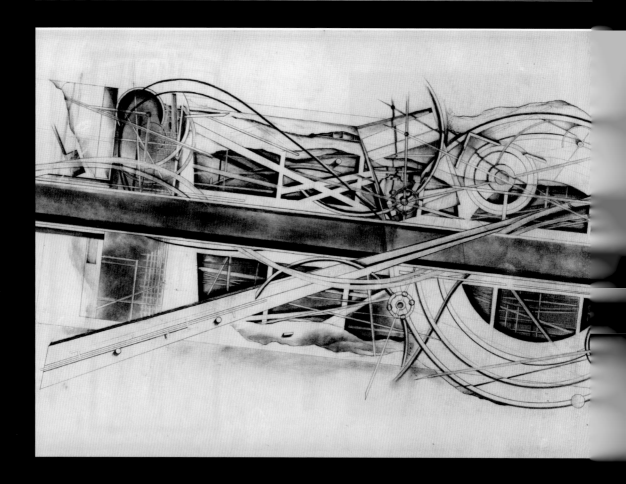

description This project is located in an abandoned train tunnel built in the early 1900s, an important industrial portal between New York and New Jersey. In early 1987, the Tunnel Dance Club was built on the site and the abandoned train tunnel became the main dance floor. It was one of the most distinctive dance clubs of its time, featuring unisex bathrooms that were partially converted locker rooms. Before closing in 2001, the Tunnel was a center for 1980s culture and nightlife. The Museum of Transit History will reintroduce this unique urban space to the city. The main exhibition area will be housed in the tunnel, and the interior core of the old building will be exposed for viewing.

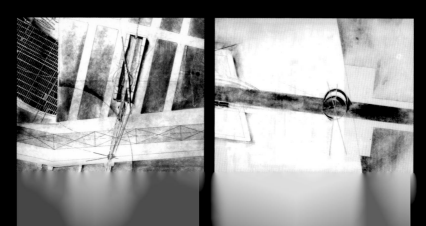

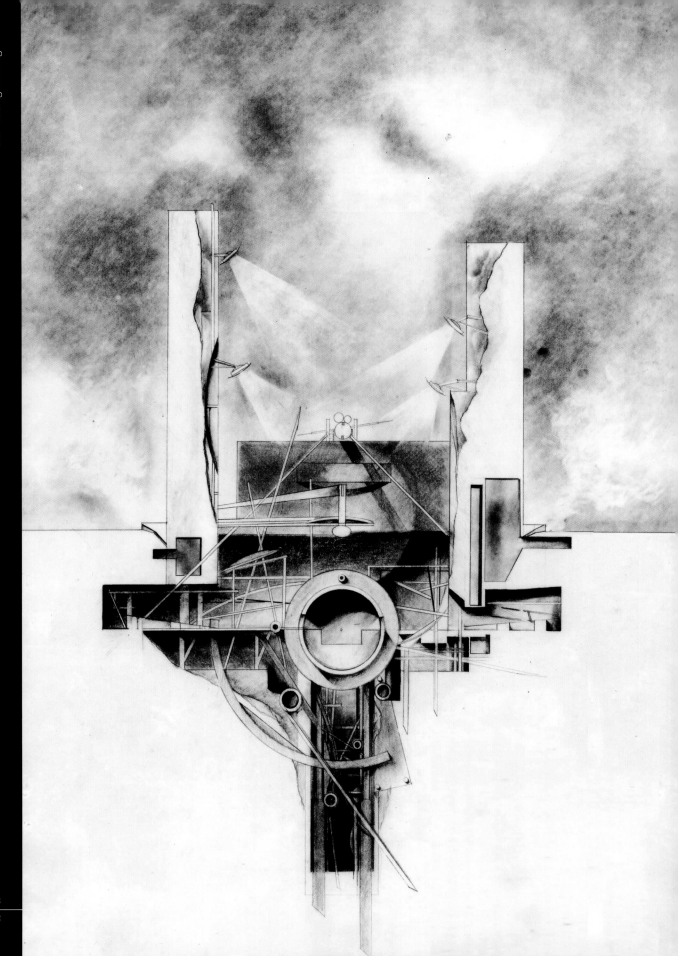

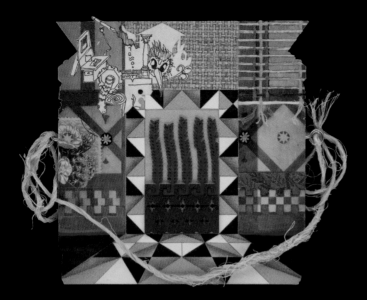

Timothy Collins

Müllschützengräben
(Trash Trench/Waste Trenches)

description   Architects use drawing to construct spaces. Similarly, these collages attempt to rebuild memory and create landscapes to inhabit. Drawing is an exploration, as both map and territory. And, as the map is being invented, the journey is taking place. Therefore, the work of "art" is what remains from the dérive: a stilled-life section of the process of visualization. Each piece is a kind of "thinking-table" upon which tandem ideas about war and the artifact intersect. Collage is a logic used to create transmutations when these fragments are joined. Dada critiqued the mechanized madness of World War I by co-opting its illusions of scientific precision to expose the latent absurdity and impotence of modern warfare. Technology was revealed to amplify the barbarism and inhumanity of society.

Timothy Matthew Collins
?=?=?
Five War Poems

Shrapnel comes
as surely as the sun
on clear mornings
piercing the stiff air
with ferocious physics:
a deadly concoction
of will and chance
colliding in the abdomen
or temple of the soldier
whose presence is statistic
intersected with horror
and grief driven down
into rock and mud
silently computing nomore.
White hot
blue nostrils stained
putrid, un-relenting chaos:
a graveyard battered
by steel behemoths
into uncouth husks
of rock, tree, and dust.
Scales of the Heart's disease

Barbs
TANGLE WEBLORN
CRUCIFIXING THE DEW
IN DROPLETS SANGUINE
AMID RIFLES REPEATING:
*Sn-sn-rrn gases blistering skin
are those thorns penance for our sins?*

A Living Tomb
is where I lay
putting out water
deep by day.

Relief will come
by Christmas they say,
but I can't imagine
living till then

for the bache are
Preciously
covering our cuts,
METHODICALLY

The earth was like some putrid tundra desolating our eyes as we jumped back into the
trenches whose sorry state, I'm sad to say, was little more comforting, what with its shattered
revels like ruptured arrow heads ready to skewer anyone who fell by accident, and the
poisoned water at our sewer feet, rank with feces and all manner of things. The earth is dead
and we, as far as I am concerned, are lined up in a living tomb, waiting for the order to charge,
waiting for the sting of hot steel, waiting for the thundering, upturned dirt to settle under our raging KA-BARing forward
feet so we might at last rise to become entangled in barbed wire or mowed down like so many departing shades ever-facing
matchsticks. I pray you never visit the Somme, or Verdun, because even in hoped-for times of a no-win won for ungrateful eyes
peace, these lands will lay fallow with so many young corpses rotting at the roots, judging sacrifice in so simple terms.

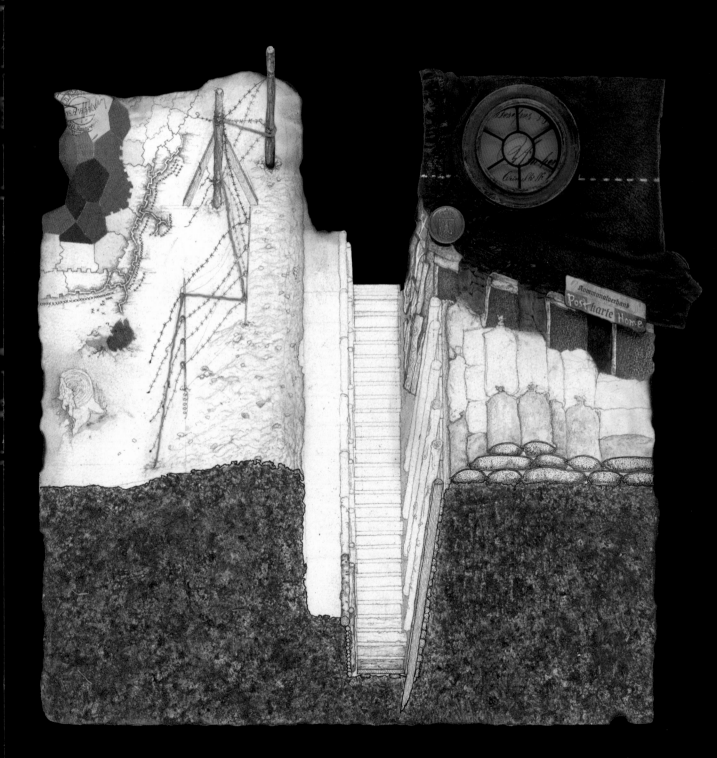

Villa D'Este

NATURE AND ART ARE RICHLY COMBINED IN THIS FO

THE SET CONSISTS OF FIVE STRIPS, EACH 28 INCHES WIDE AND 10 FEET HIGH, AND THREE ROLLS O
FIVE STRIPS COVER 11 FEET 8 INCHES OF WALLSPACE. THE SET COVERS A WALL OF AVERAGE HEIGHT
HIGHEST POINT OF DESIGN IS 60 INCHES, WITH 36 INCHES OF PLAIN GROUND BELOW THE DESIGN

STYLE # VI-830

11'8"

$96.00 PER SET ON SILK TEXTURED WALLPAPER
ADDITIONAL SILK TEXTURED PLAIN WALLPAPER FOR ADJOINING WALLS:
$3.95 PER ROLL

Johanna Dickson

Brunswick School Greenwich, CT
Firm: Skidmore Owings & Merrill
Master's Thesis University of Pennsylvania

description These pages: This project with SOM is an addition and renovation to a high school for boys in Greenwich. A new link was created between five existing buildings (and six different floor levels) through a glass and steel pedestrian walkway. An existing gymnasium was converted into an auditorium and additional performance spaces. • Following pages: My thesis studied the application of methods for the treatment of Post-Traumatic Stress Disorder, at the site of the 1985 MOVE bombing in Philadelphia. The project was selected for its own edition of Pamphlet Architecture (#23).

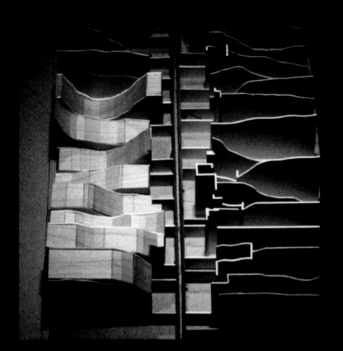

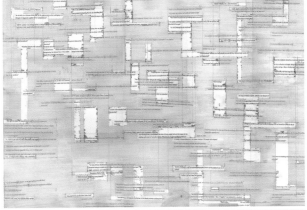

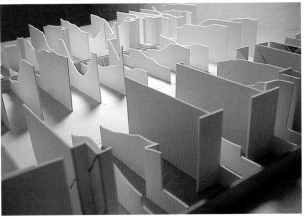

Antonio Di Oronzo

Lake June Pointe House
Lake Placid, Florida

description The clarity, color and shape of the lake and sky, the orange grove, and the sand of the site itself are dynamic entities that adjust and interact with one another. The three volumes appear to slide along with the shifting nature. • Its overall shape is elongated and oriented to maximize use of daylight. The floor plans are organized to take advantage of cross ventilation, a simple and effective ecological precept that Florida architecture used to follow before air conditioning became mainstream. • With a budget of $80 per square-foot, this 3,200 square foot, 3-bedroom house transcends the upscale setting of the gated lakefront community by demonstrating that being environmentally sound building does not have to be expensive.

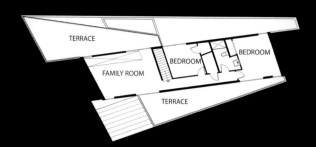

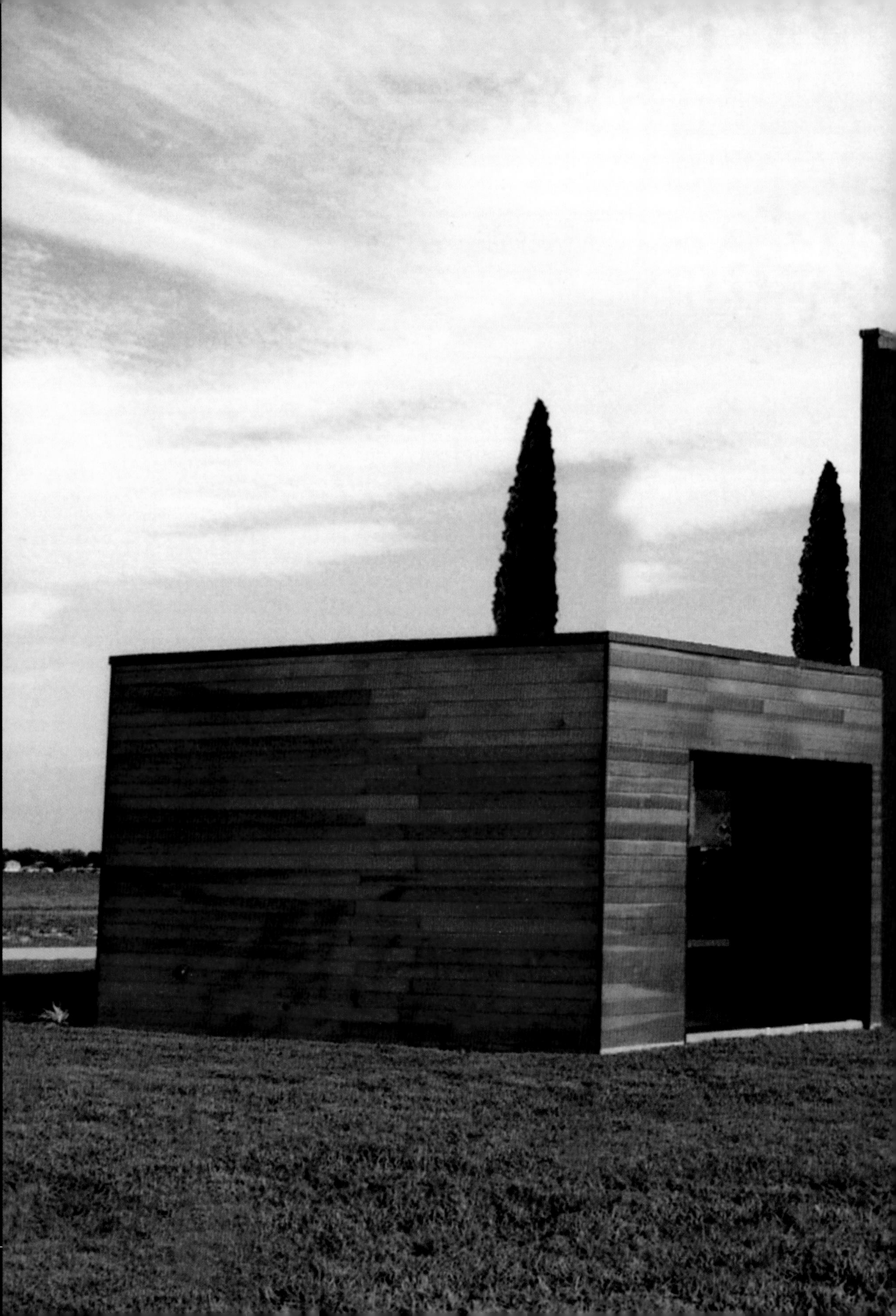

Jeremy Edmiston

2009 aA SHELTER
New York City
Firm: SYSTEMarchitects

description 2009 aA SHELTER is a 4,000 square foot room that is used as a multi-purpose space for the All Angels Church on the upper west side to run their homeless outreach activities. As a not-for-profit institution, they have run a homeless shelter in the city since the church was established in Seneca Village over 180 years ago. The elements of the space: floor, operable wall and ceiling, test a geometry of pathways that both curve and fold. Everyone follows their own path, and the lines and curves form a unity that articulates the nuances of each person's engagement with the relationships we need to maintain to coexist in the city. Geometry and pattern resolve the use of the space with the idealism of public service.

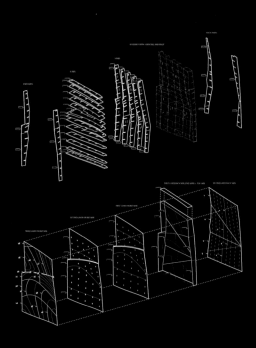
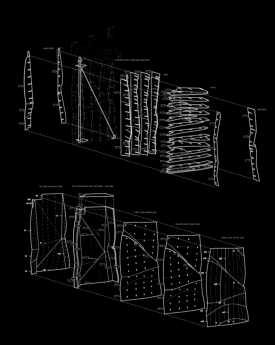

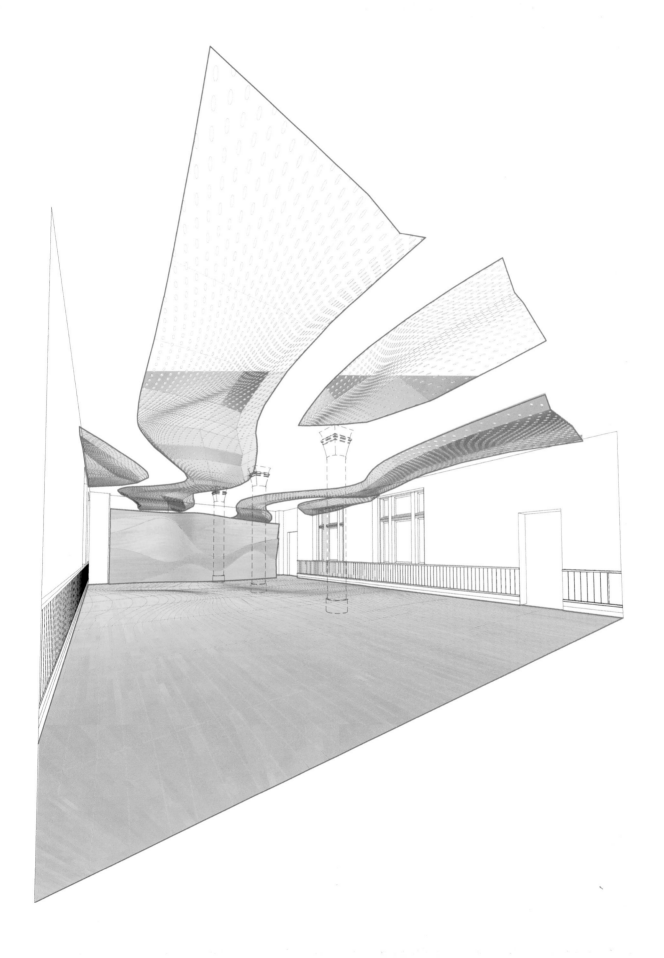

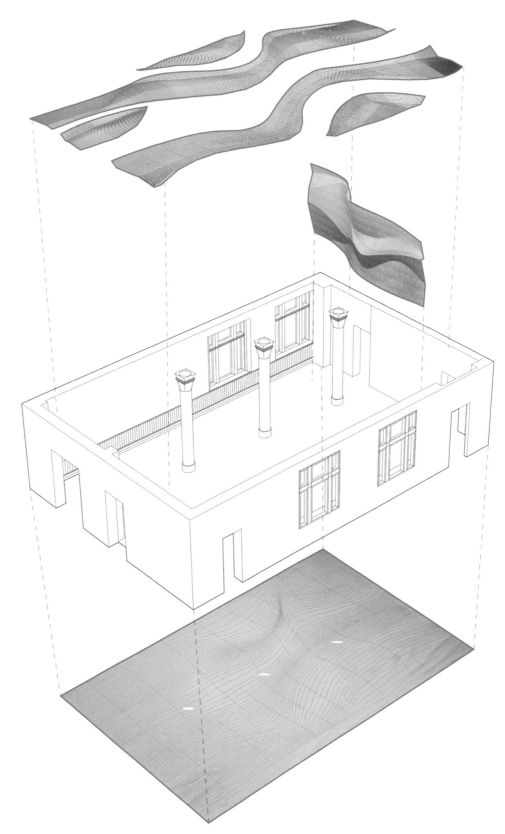

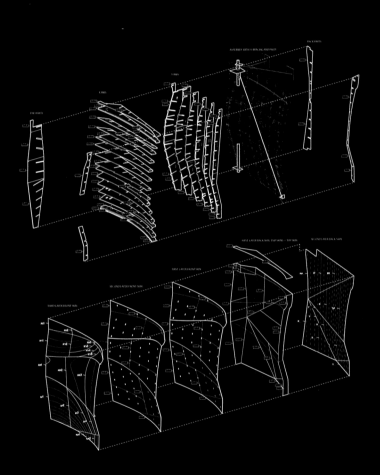

Alan Feigenberg

Patterns: In and Of
Architecture

description As an architect and a photographer, I observe and read the world through patterns: in design, materials, methods, and the process of construction. In these photos of varying aspects of the construction process, the storing and preparation of materials, or the ordering of materials, I reflect and develop my perspective in the extension of these patterns onto the matt, as reinforcement, or as contradiction of the photographed image. ● In the three-dimensional projects the structure is a given, a series of frames within a frame with its inherent pattern of boxes/spaces. The wood pieces are armatures; the encasements and the parameters for bringing together the images that would otherwise not occur in "real" architecture.

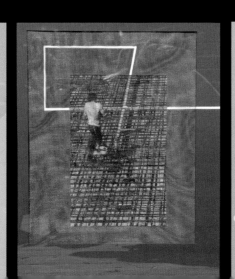

Alberto Foyo

Dacha Cartouche
Jefferson, Schoharie County, New York

description An earthwork that includes a one-acre body of water and a one thousand square feet dwelling. The project was nicknamed "cooking with what is there". Underground aquifers and blue clay subsoil provided the essential materials to build the pond. Stone walls crisscrossing the land provided the inspiration and the anchoring of the house to the site. The contours of the pond were designed to bring the existing evergreens (mainly spruces) to the foreground and to maximize their mirroring in the water. Contours act as curvilinear vectors that intertwine the horizontality of the pond with the verticality of the trees, thus defining a natural courtyard. The vectors establish a system of vanishing points that release the pressure of the forest.

carport

studiolo

cubiculum
nocturnum

g a l e r i a

cloister-patio

shower

sauna

barbeque

bridge

loft

perch

verandah-pergola

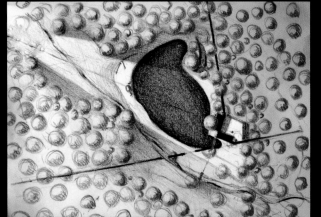

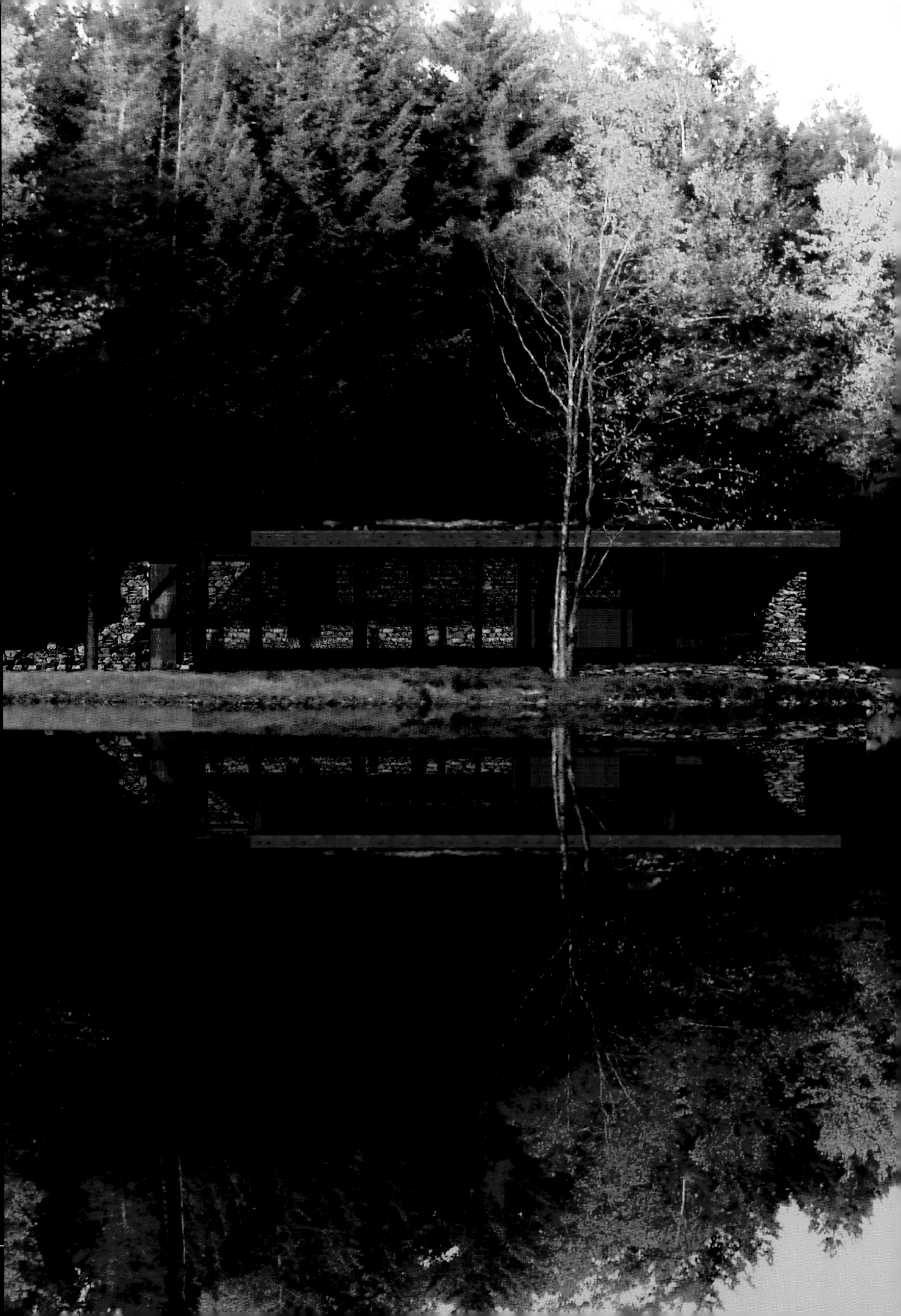

Athanasios Haritos

Achio House
San Jose, Costa Rica
In collaboration with Guillermo Garita

description Achio House is located in San Jose, Costa Rica, in the Rio de Oro residential development, a setting comprised of sporadic low-scale dwellings. The house sought to reconcile various factors of program, site and technology and to achieve a meaningful existence with its surroundings. A linear translucent bar defines and screens the south edge boundary line. A periphery wall secures the property and stabilizes the geometry of the site. The ground plan of the house is set in oblique orientation to the site and touches the north boundary wall, reconciling the plan to the property and recalling distant views of the context. A linear translucent bar defines and screens the south edge boundary line

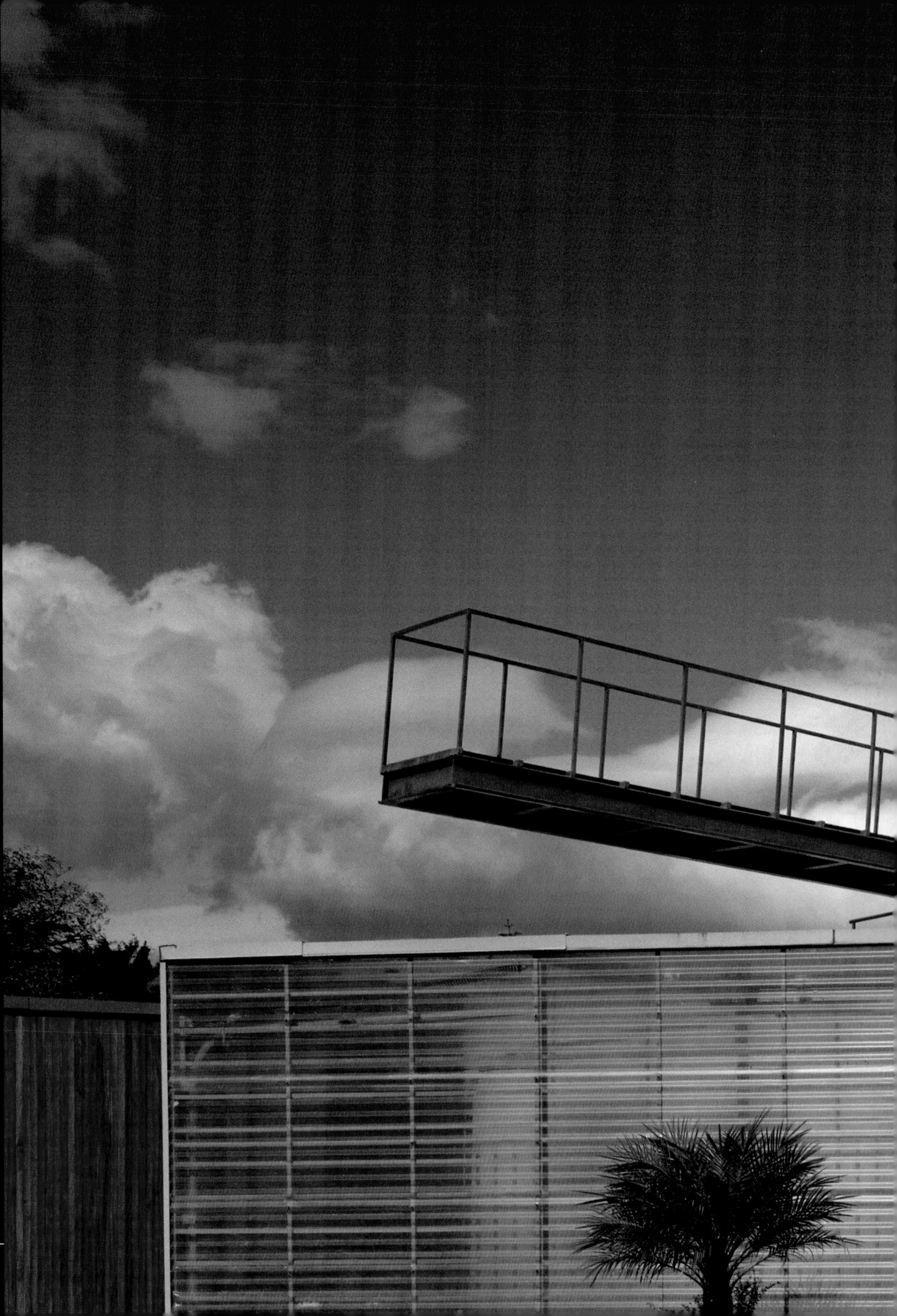

Ghislaine Hermanuz

African Square
Harlem, New York

description African Square, at the intersection of 125th Street and 7th Avenue, has historically been the setting of major cultural, political and community events in Harlem. Black leaders, including A. Philip Randolph, Malcolm X, and Nelson Mandela, have addressed Harlem from there. Creating a design for the plaza is a unique opportunity for Harlem to take ownership of the historical legacy embedded in the site. The new plaza celebrates the community's collective memory by interpreting it in brick and mortar, grounding the design in the principles of traditional African public spaces, while telling the story of the community. Built from Harlem's memories and its African roots, the Plaza will become a relevant historical marker.

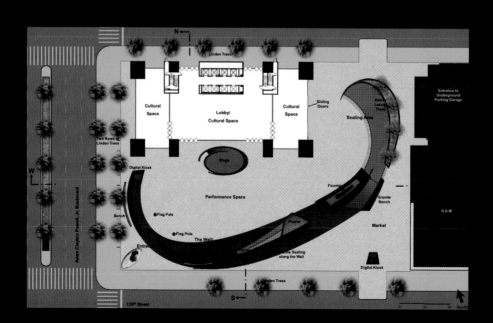

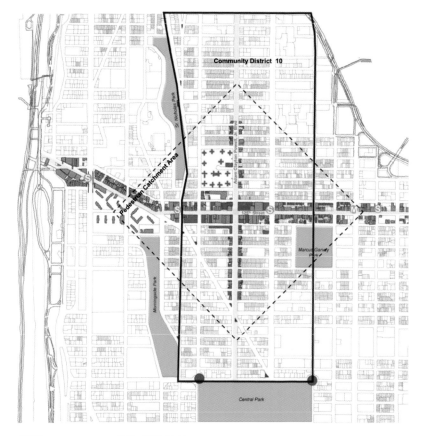

Public Plazas   **Neighborhood Landmarks**

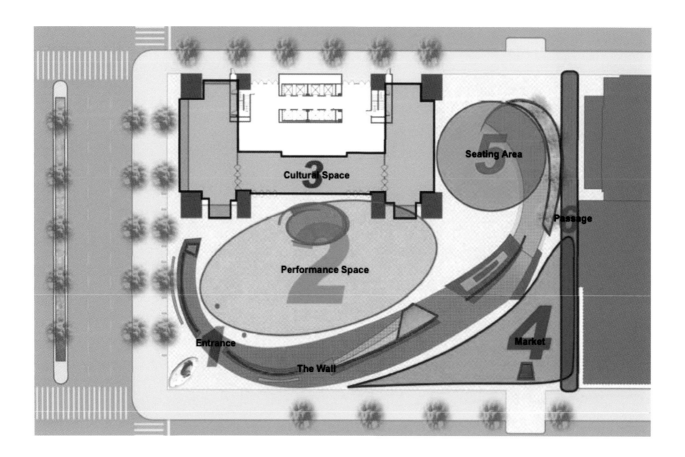

Cultural Space **3**

Seating Area **5**

Performance Space **2**

Passage **6**

Entrance **1**

The Wall

Market **4**

AFRICAN SQUARE: TRANSFORMATION OF THE PLAZA
Adam Clayton Powell, Jr. State Office Building Plaza Planning and Design

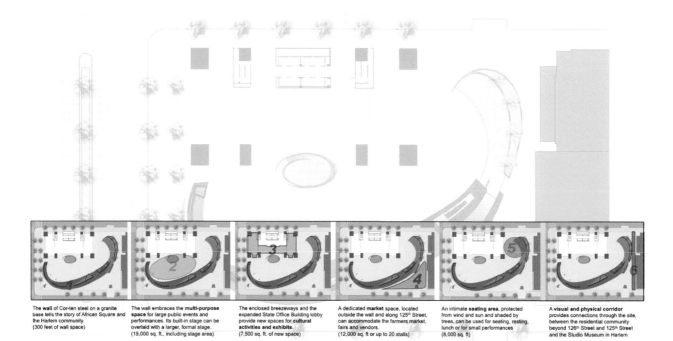

The **wall** of Cor-ten steel on a granite base tells the story of African Square and the Harlem community.
(300 feet of wall space)

The wall embraces the **multi-purpose space** for large public events and performances. Its built-in stage can be overlaid with a larger, formal stage.
(19,000 sq. ft., including stage area)

The enclosed breezeways and the expanded State Office Building lobby provide new spaces for **cultural activities and exhibits.**
(7,500 sq. ft. of new space)

A dedicated **market** space, located outside the wall and along 125th Street, can accommodate the farmers market, fairs and vendors.
(12,000 sq. ft or up to 20 stalls)

An intimate **seating area**, protected from wind and sun and shaded by trees, can be used for seating, resting, lunch or for small performances
(8,000 sq. ft)

A **visual and physical corridor** provides connections through the site, between the residential community beyond 126th Street and 125th Street and the Studio Museum in Harlem

Ali C. Höcek

Sana'a Terraces
Yemen

description Sana'a Terraces is a high-end residential gated community comprised of a mix of estate villas, standard villas, townhouses and apartments. The area will support a community that may serve foreign dignitaries and investors that are seeking an exclusive, slightly removed residential location that has direct access to key destinations. The sloping site is located at the base of the mountain, with commanding view of the entire city of Sana'a and mountainous landscape features: ravines, peaks and rock formations. Each of the four housing typologies will have unique requirements and character, and unique market niche and buyer profile. The building structure is a modular kit of parts that can be reconfigured in different patterns.

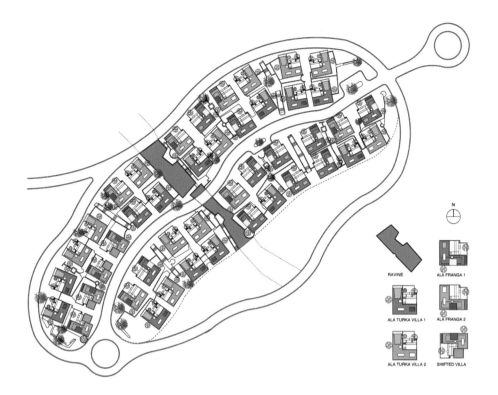

N

RAVINE

ALA FRANGA 1

ALA TURKA VILLA 1

ALA FRANGA 2

ALA TURKA VILLA 2

SHIFTED VILLA

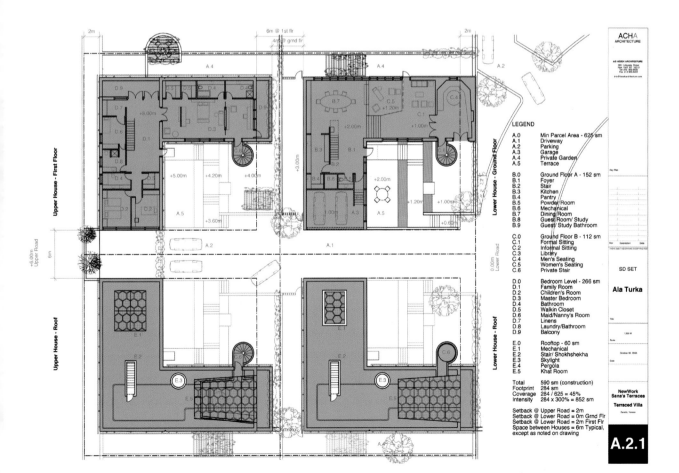

Upper House - First Floor

Lower House - Ground Floor

Upper House - Roof

Lower House - Roof

2m

6m @ 1st flr
4m @ grnd flr

2m

A.4

A.4

A.2

A.2

+8.00m

+5.00m   +4.20m   +4.00m

+3.60m

+5.00m

+3.00m

+2.00m

+2.00m

+1.20m   +1.00m

+1.20m   +1.00m

+0.60m

+6.00m
Upper Road

6m

0.00m
Lower Road

A.2

A.1

E.1

E.2

E.3

E.2

E.3

ACHA
ARCHITECTURE

AD HODEK ARCHITECTURE

LEGEND

A.0	Min Parcel Area - 625 sm
A.1	Driveway
A.2	Parking
A.3	Garage
A.4	Private Garden
A.5	Terrace
B.0	Ground Floor A - 152 sm
B.1	Foyer
B.2	Stair
B.3	Kitchen
B.4	Pantry
B.5	Powder Room
B.6	Mechanical
B.7	Dining Room
B.8	Guest/ Room/ Study
B.9	Guest/ Study Bathroom
C.0	Ground Floor B - 112 sm
C.1	Formal Sitting
C.2	Informal Sitting
C.3	Library
C.4	Men's Seating
C.5	Women's Seating
C.6	Private Stair
D.0	Bedroom Level - 266 sm
D.1	Family Room
D.2	Children's Room
D.3	Master Bedroom
D.4	Bathroom
D.5	Walkin Closet
D.6	Maid/Nanny's Room
D.7	Linens
D.8	Laundry/Bathroom
D.9	Balcony
E.0	Rooftop - 60 sm
E.1	Mechanical
E.2	Stair/ Shokhshekha
E.3	Skylight
E.4	Pergola
E.5	Khat Room

Total   590 sm (construction)
Footprint   284 sm
Coverage   284 / 625 = 45%
Intensity   284 x 300% = 852 sm

Setback @ Upper Road = 2m
Setback @ Lower Road = 0m Grnd Flr
Setback @ Lower Road = 2m First Flr
Space between Houses = 6m Typical,
except as noted on drawing

Key Map

SD SET

Ala Turka

NewWork
Sana'a Terraces

Terraced Villa

A.2.1

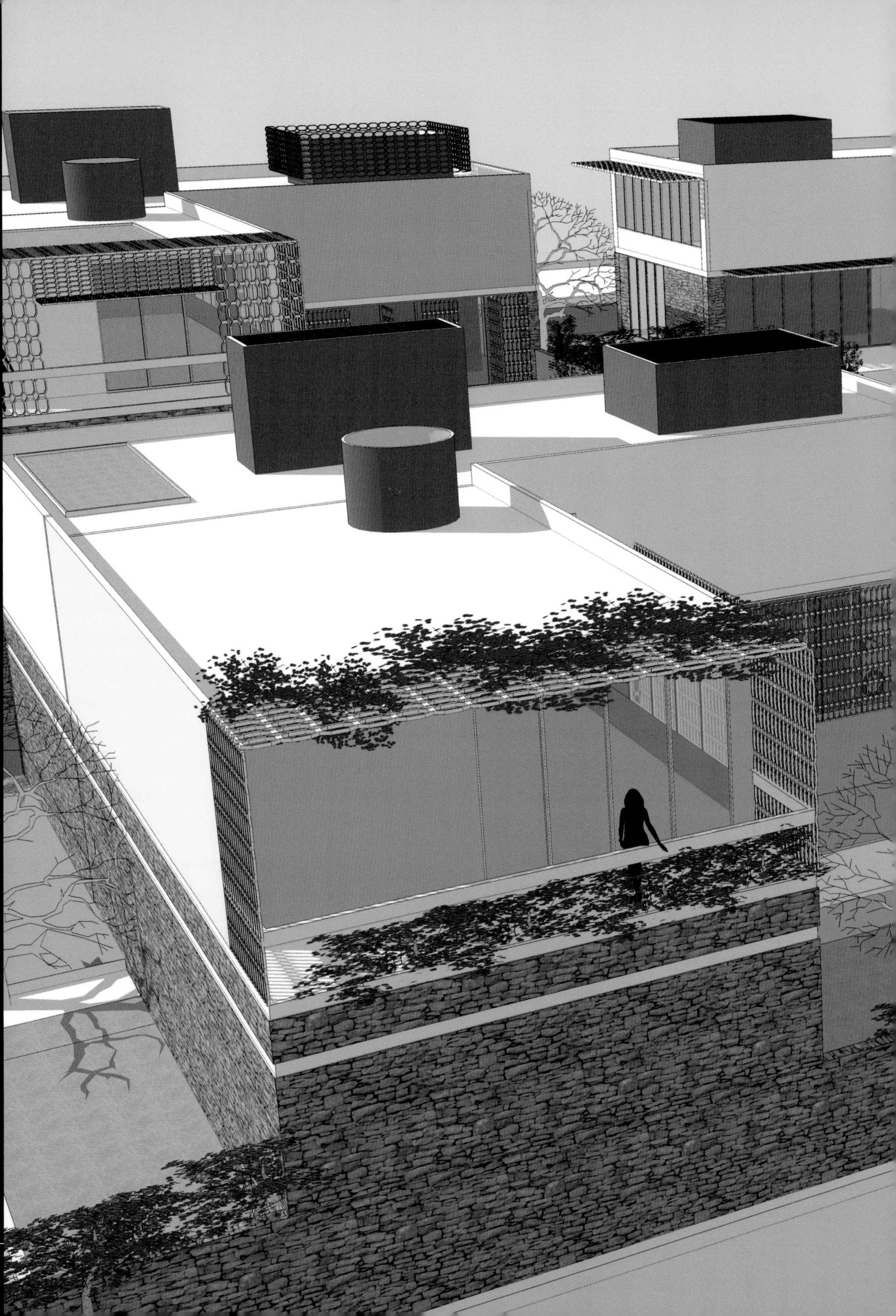

description The meta-park, or comprehensive design for the urban landscape, offers potential to lower atmospheric carbon concentration levels through sequestration of carbon in plant and soil systems. Reframing the urban landscape as an apparatus for ecological recovery will empower citizens to actively engage the issue of global warming. Reframing urban planting with an operative environmental program, as opposed to deploying planting as scenographic device, will combat the perception that cities are un-natural and reciprocally, that nature is un-urban.

LINE SINK: highway sound bio-barrier retrofit

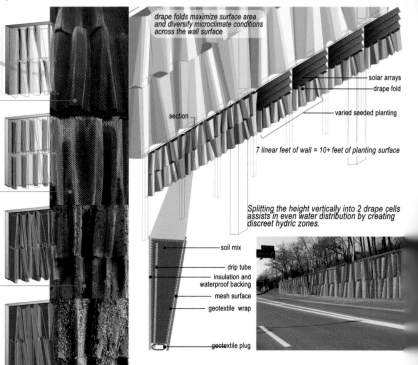

Drape retrofit panels are 2-ply steel mesh, with formed and tied off folds for the outer ply. The deep profile enables cladding of existing concrete walls with columns of soil mix to sustain robust biomass. Mesh folds create shade and vertical zones of wind protection. The horizontal split enhances micro-condition diversity and ease of hanging.

folds are 9-12 inches deep

A soil mix fills the columnar gaps created by the folds. Geo-fabric retains the mix within the metal drape. The soil is designed to retain moisture - hydrogel? Engineering soil mixes to sustain soil processes in urban conditions is premiated over engineering plant system technologies for architectural efficiency. The thick profile decreases weathering impacts.

soil tube inside

Netafim drip irrigation tubing snakes through the columns; and once the drape is ready for planting, it is turned on to saturate the soil mix. Accessing highway runoff for irrigation (filtered and powered by solar panels) constructs a sustainable highway ecology. Soil fibers should expand through the mesh to provide a porous surface for seeding. This interface is critical to propagate seedlings and to establish rooting for C transfer into soil.

soil penetrates face of mesh folds

The drapes can be hand-seeded, scrape mix into the mesh, or possibly hydro-seeded with appropriate low emission vehicles. Seed mixes containing alpine perennials, mixed perennial short grasses or perennial vines could be sustained - the key is to seed a range of material that can form adapted patches in the varied environment of the drape folds.

seed adheres to porous surface

upper panel
lower panel

drape folds maximize surface area and diversify microclimate conditions across the wall surface

solar arrays
drape fold

section

varied seeded planting

7 linear feet of wall = 10+ feet of planting surface

Splitting the height vertically into 2 drape cells assists in even water distribution by creating discreet hydric zones.

soil mix
drip tube
insulation and waterproof backing
mesh surface
geotextile wrap

geotextile plug

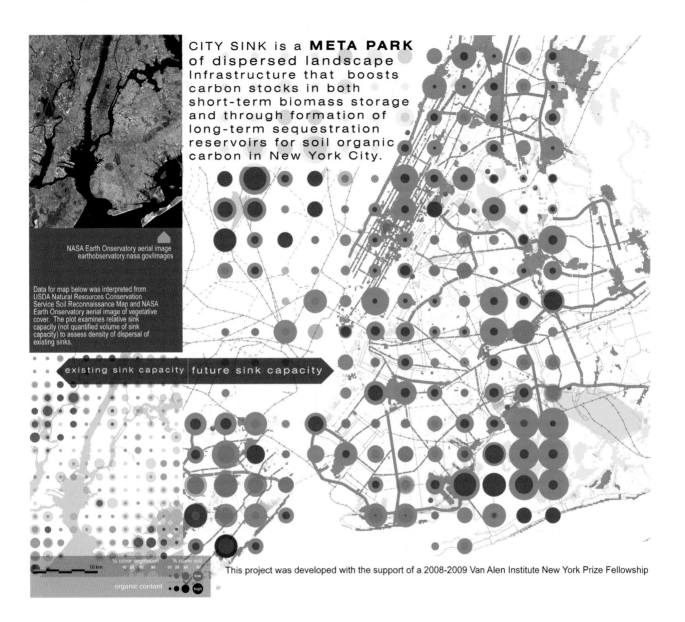

CITY SINK is a **META PARK** of dispersed landscape Infrastructure that boosts carbon stocks in both short-term biomass storage and through formation of long-term sequestration reservoirs for soil organic carbon in New York City.

NASA Earth Onservatory aerial image
earthobservatory.nasa.gov/images

Data for map below was interpreted from USDA Natural Resources Conservation Service Soil Reconnaissance Map and NASA Earth Onservatory aerial image of vegetative cover. The plot examines relative sink capacity (not quantified volume of sink capacity) to assess density of dispersal of existing sinks.

existing sink capacity | future sink capacity

10 km

% cover vegetation 10 25 50 90 | % cover soil 10 25 50 90 low

organic content ● ● ● high

This project was developed with the support of a 2008-2009 Van Alen Institute New York Prize Fellowship

QUEENS FIELDS - the view from the el

Views from elevated rail lines drive the image of the greenroof sinks. Greenroofs are opportunities to create public spaces from unused private terrain.

first year seed scatter: each symbol represents one seed per 100 at installation in a random broadcast

green symbols indicate grasses and perennial species that bloom the second year

second year and beyond: grasses expand, perennials bloom, colonies of reseeded annuals and stoloniferous perennials take shape

FIELD SINK: green(roof) fields

high - consistently dry
slope - can be dry, needs rootmat
low - wetter, slightly sheltered

A shallow intensive green roof system can enable retrofit of existing structures to support habitat-capacity or agricultural planting with a load rate similar to an extensive greenroof that is limited to a monoculture of sedum.

Zones of Intense Competition - upslope/downslope species battle it out based on unique tolerances

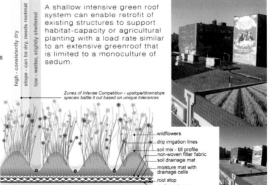

wildflowers
drip irrigation lines
soil mix - till profile
non-woven filter fabric
soil drainage mat
moisture mat with drainage cells
root stop
roof membrane

interspecies competition and commensal relations animate green roof fields

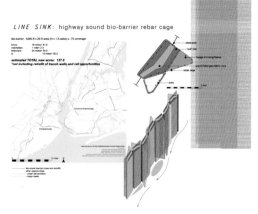

LINE SINK: highway sound bio-barrier rebar cage

bio-barrier: 5280 ft x 25 ft area (H x 1.5-sides) x .75 coverage

bronx   18 miles= 41.0
manhattan   1 mile= 2.3
brooklyn   24 miles= 54.5
si   13 miles= 30.0

estimated TOTAL new acres: 127.8
*not including retrofit of trench walls and rail opportunities

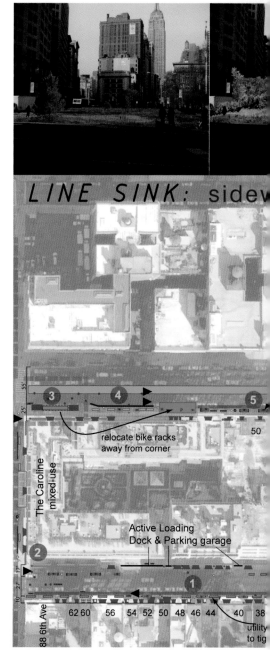

LINE SINK: sidew

The Caroline
mixed-use

relocate bike racks
away from corner

Active Loading
Dock & Parking garage

55

25

50

3   4   5

2

1

10 27 17

88 6th Ave   62 60   56   54 52 50   48 46 44   40   38

utility
to tig

street strips

The Flatiron neighborhood was used as a case study to play out sink dispersal tactics and implications for urban landscape design. The map below documents existing obstructions to street trees and opportunities for the sidewalk and strip sink network.

frastructure
d strips with benches
d strips with street guard
ade layered strips - street trees with shrubs
ade strips with benches
ade strips with street guard
ade strips
parking sink
t strip

► projected views

100 ft

augment
ree pits

infill plantings create
pockets of density

one lane strip

32   26 24 22 20 18 16 14

ome Depot

Active Loading Dock

30   16   Parking Lot

Flat Iron Building

55'
23'

12' 27.5' 10'
15'

Madison Square Park

existing parks are
woven into sinks by accretion
► or expansion

9

10

15'

10' 15'

Mixed Use   10 - 12 14

sinks berm-up over
structure to create tree pits

11

6   7   8

Lewis Iglehart

Illustrations, Interior, Graphics

1. Tellers Restaurant, Huntington, NY (DETAIL)
   Design: Soffes Wood Design LLC
2. North Fork Bank East 59th. St.,
   NYC Design: JRS Architects, NY, NY
3. Poseidon's Light Design Graphic
4, 5, 6. Galerie au Chocolat
   Cincinnati, Ohio
   Retail Interior
   Design: Iglehart & Struhs, Architects
   Photos: Walter Vosberg
7. Windows Design Graphic
8. Windows Design Graphic

3

4

5

6

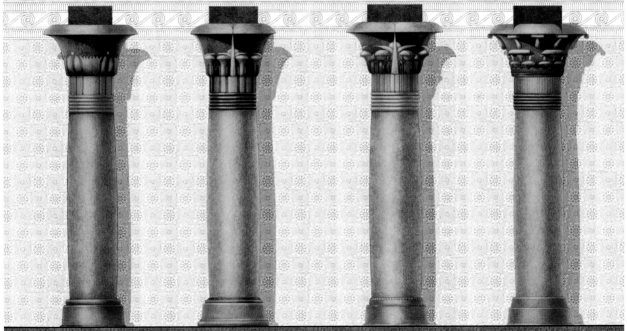

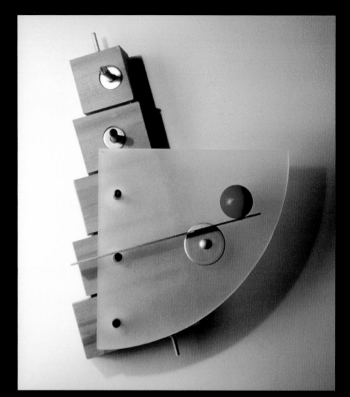

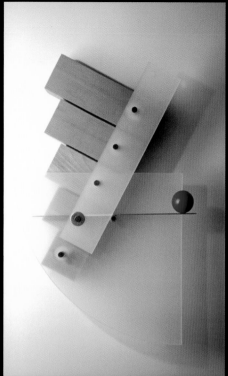

David Judelson

Sculptures

description My sculpture is informed by my background in architecture and my interest in construction, structure and materials. • Reconstructed Circle is fabricated using the forces of tension, compression and bending to structurally reconstitute the quadrants of a circle, constructed of aircraft cable, rubber tubing and plywood. The pieces from the Zoning Envelope series and the Weights and Measures series, made of cedar blocks, sanded plexiglass, aluminum and steel hardware and a signature red ball, explore issues of composition and balance. • Critic Robert Campbell of the Boston Globe compared the sculptures to the drawings of Rube Goldberg, describing the work as "successful at making visible the hidden forces of tension and compression."

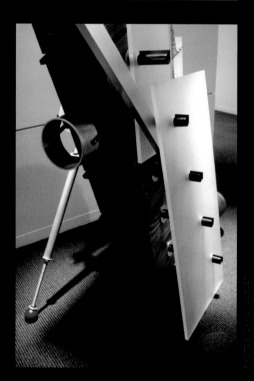

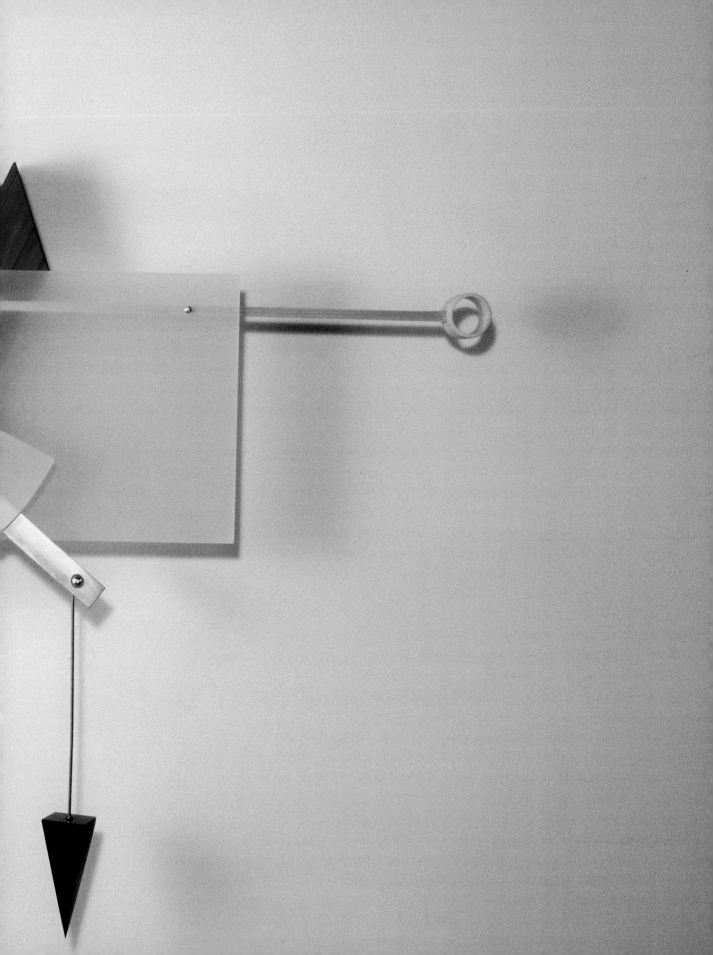

Vanessa Keith

description Located in Manhattan's Flatiron District, this 3,100 square foot space for an innovative, cutting edge marketing firm is a different take on the urban workplace. The project combines spaces for creative work that allow multiple opportunities for chance happenings and cross fertilization. The entry is framed on one side by a curved DJ booth and waiting area, and on the other by a reception area. The DJ booth found its way into the project when the design team discovered that the company founder had been a DJ in his youth, travelling widely and performing with a number of well known acts. He wanted a space that would reflect the youthful energy of the company, a place to work, but also one informal enough to hang out in and spin a few tracks.

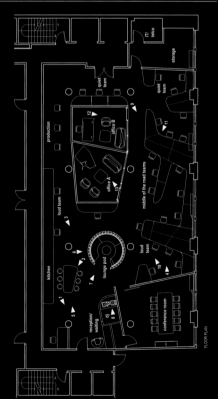

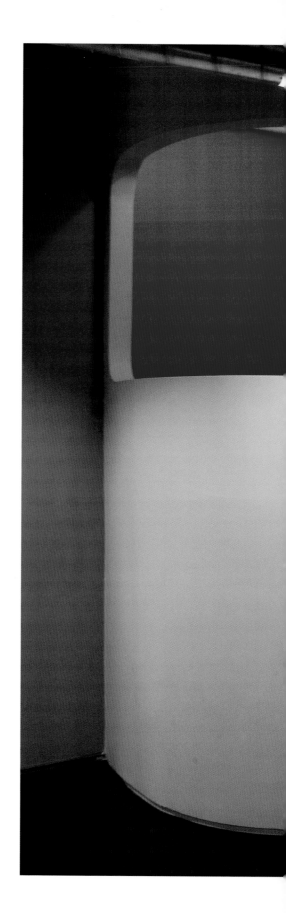

Fran Leadon

Fragment
Brooklyn, New York

description For the last two years, I have been documenting the attempted demolition of 624 Pacific Street in Brooklyn, a four-story apartment building in the footprint of the proposed Atlantic Yards development. No. 624 was originally one in a line of typical background buildings that defines the street and provide a sense of scale to Brooklyn's neighborhoods. Now it sits alone in a field of rubble. • The neighborhood, between Fort Greene, Prospect Heights, and Park Slope, is a thriving and diverse community, but Atlantic Yards developer Forest City Ratner convinced the city to declare the area "blighted" and began demolition, creating a series of forlorn vacant lots. The recent economic downturn has delayed further construction, and No. 624 remains (for now).

PHOTOS SAM FENTRESS AND FABIAN LLONCH

Fabian Llonch

Rock Bridge Christian Church
Columbia, Missouri

description The program called for a new sanctuary, classrooms, and narthex to be built as an addition to two existing buildings. • The project became a free spirit occupying the space between the buildings, like a flowing wind contrasted against the rigidity of the existing structures. We proposed two arms, embracing the site, program, and community: one arm (the sanctuary) at the same level as the main entrance and a second arm (the classrooms) sloping down with the existing topography. As a site strategy, two exterior pathways will run through the site, like rivers, as an open invitation for different people to gather. The blending of the pathways with the new building will create two distinct outer spaces.

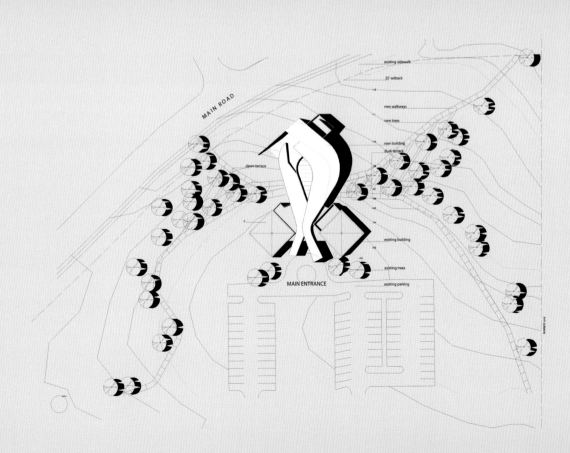

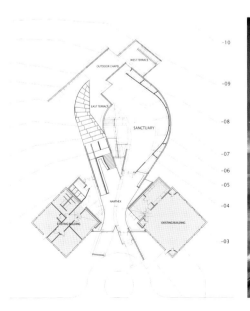

Peter Lynch

House for an Industrialist
Shenzhen, China
In collaboration with Ahlaiya Yung

description We are completing the interior renovation of a 5000 square foot villa that embodies new ideas about craft, geometry and ornament for a steel industrialist in Shenzhen. Installations on the ceilings, floors, and walls are built up of custom-fabricated repetitive elements: sculptural ceramic tiles, anodized aluminum branches, lacquered hardwood spindles and woven rattan panels. Hundreds of these elements are arranged in non-repetitive, self-structuring patterns. The visitor's experience unfolds musically. One theme that emerge is the dome: from the entry vestibule to the most private spaces, various types of domes are encountered. The project demonstrates the high skill level of Chinese craftspeople.

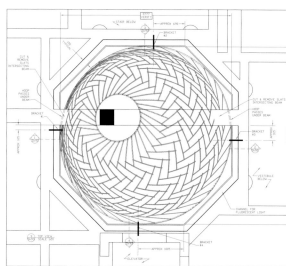

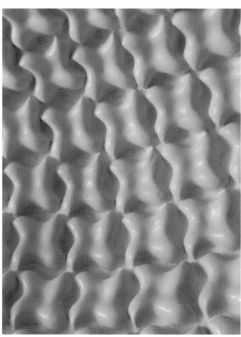

Irma Ostroff

1. Watercolor
2. Color 16
3. Color 18
4. Excavation, 22nd Street
5. Figure 2
6. Remember Me
7. Back 1

description I've kept FUN and slowly shed FORM in two-dimensional works that use various drawing and painting media to play with and/or explore color, pattern, process, and perception.

5

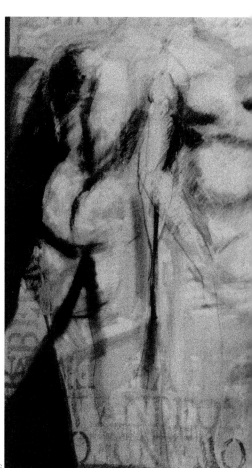

6

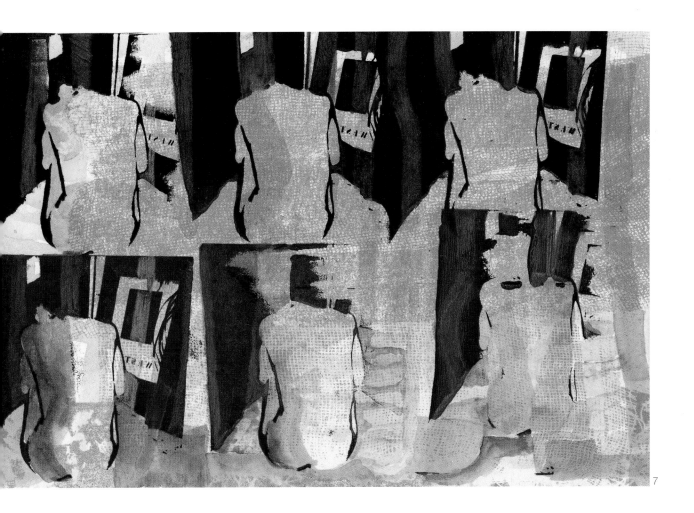

7

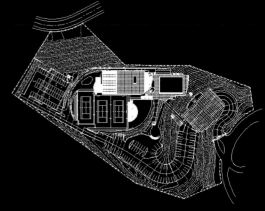

Ivan Rosa

Valle Arriba Athletic Club
Caracas, Venezuela
Firm: Hillier Architecture

description This project was the winning entry in an international competition that took place in 1999. The Club wanted to expand their existing fitness center and swimming facilities. The main building was to be renovated and a 30,000 square foot addition was designed incorporating a new fitness center, locker rooms, squash courts, weight rooms and restaurant. • Additional amenities included new tennis courts, a climbing wall and a natural running track.

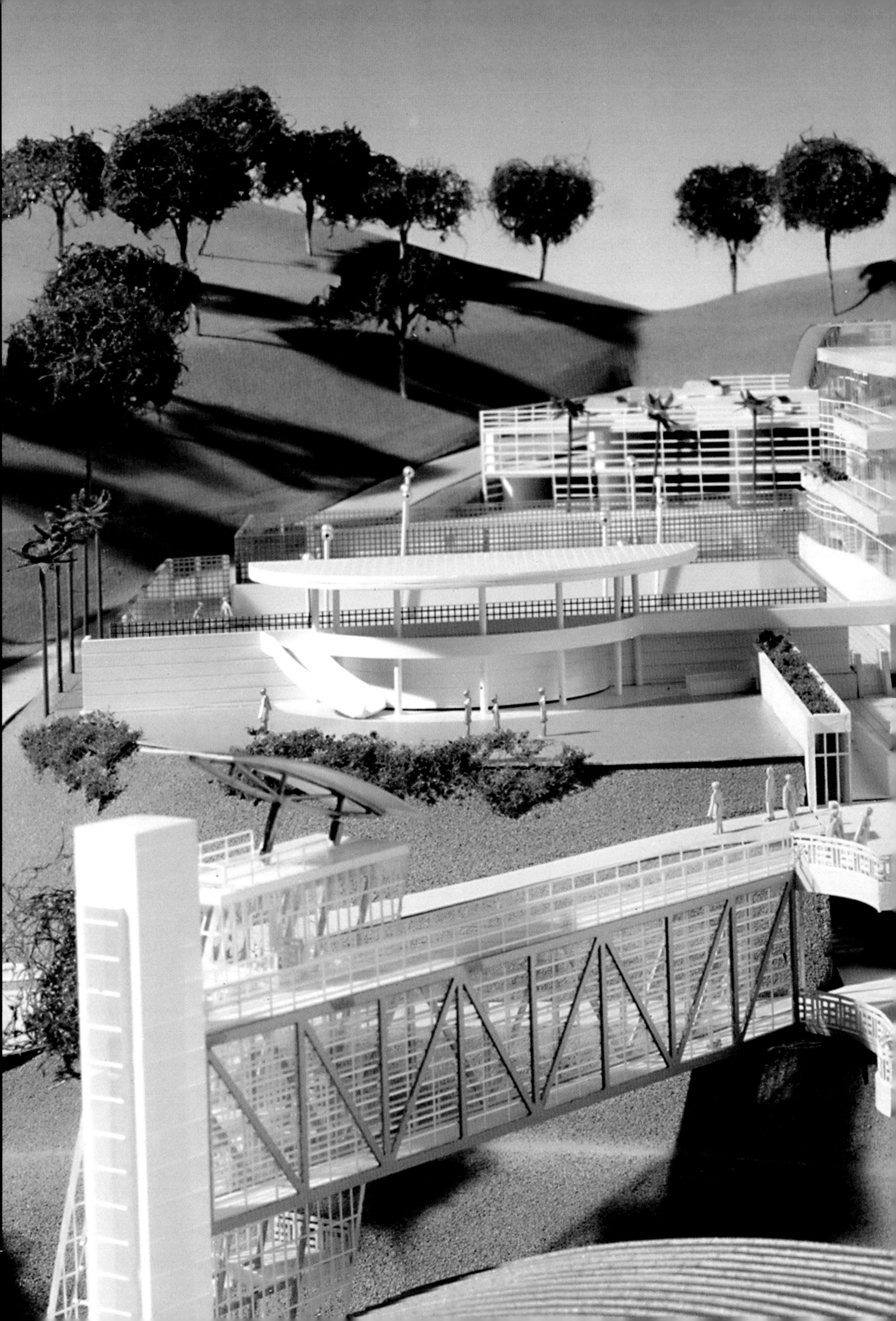

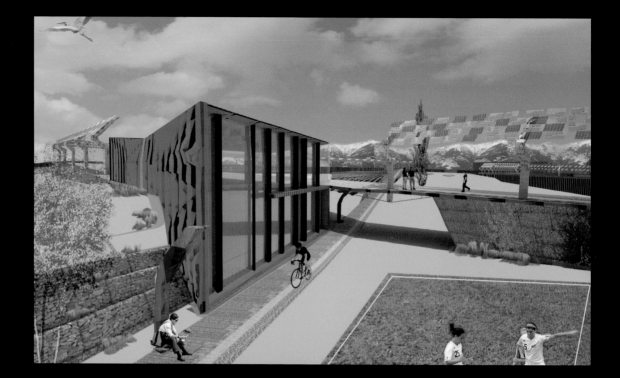

Julio Salcedo-Fernandez

description Reciprocal Areas is a link of complex relationships that promote ecology, sustainability and human activities, providing a continuum between natural and urban areas: harmonious and symbiotic interactions emerging through the creation of an infrastructure based on an internal water-cleansing loop. Storm water is collected, treated, aerated, and supplied to the urban park. The accumulated water is stored in a reserve, its borders treated as beaches and entertainment areas. Between the existing boulevards, bicycle and jogging circuit winds around the perimeter of the park.

Urban Park Valdebebas
Madrid, Spain
In collaboration with
David Fletcher,
Gema Peiro Villena

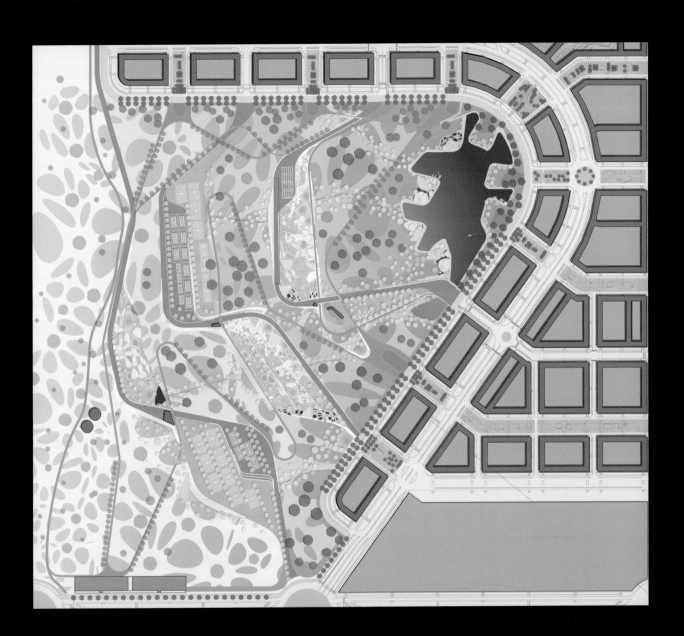

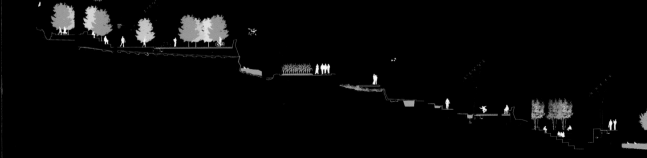

FLUJOS DE AGUA
WATER FLOWS

AGUA DE LLUVIA URBANO
STORMWATER

LAGO
LAKE

HUMEDALES ARTIFICIALES
CONSTRUCTED WETLANDS

TERRAZAS DE AGUA
WATER TERRACES

RIACHUELOS
CREEKS

RESERVA
RESERVOIR

ARROYOS
ARROYOS

FLUJOS DEL TERRENO
GOUNDPLANE FLOWS

PENÍNSULA
PENINSULA

PASEO SECUNDARIA

CIRCUITO DE RIVERA

VEREDA PRINCIPAL

MESETA

agricultural irrigation

urban runoff   biofiltration   solar-electric pumping

OLIVAR
OLIVE GROVES

PLANTACIÓN DE ALMENDROS
ALMOND GROVES

BOVEDA DE ARBOLES
TREE CANOPY

PLANTACIÓN DE ENCINAS OAK GROVES
PLANTACIÓN EN TERRA ORCHARDS
ARBOLES DE SIERRA MOUNTAIN FOREST

drinking water

treatment wetlands

greywater recycling

groundwater recharge

Michael Sorkin

Hotel Jellyfish
Tianjin, China

description This seven-star hotel is to be constructed as an iconic element in a Dubai-like development in Tianjin, China, comprising several thousand housing units, half a dozen hotels, and an extensive commercial and recreational facilities. Situated on a very large artificial lake, the hotel and two smaller private residential clubs enjoy commanding views and clean lake water for swimming. The dome atop the hotel houses bar, restaurant and private meeting and karaoke rooms. A number of both passive and active strategies are employed for energy generation and conservation, for the management of waste, and to privilege locally available labor and materials. The "legs" of the jellyfish are to be built by area shipbuilders.

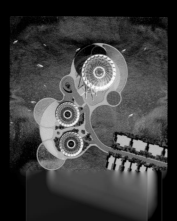

Neal Spanier

Harlem Hospital Center Modernization
Harlem, New York
Firm: HOK

description The master plan for the project integrates innovative health care planning and design excellence with the intent to express the vibrant history and culture of Harlem. The design preserves and highlights the WPA murals from existing buildings slated to be demolished and incorporates restored mural images into the building's architecture at the scale of the building's eighty foot high façade, using transparent images integrated within a sustainable high performance curtain wall. The design will increase state of the art services to the Harlem community and its surrounding neighborhoods and will advance Harlem Hospital to be one of the most technologically advanced hospitals in New York City.

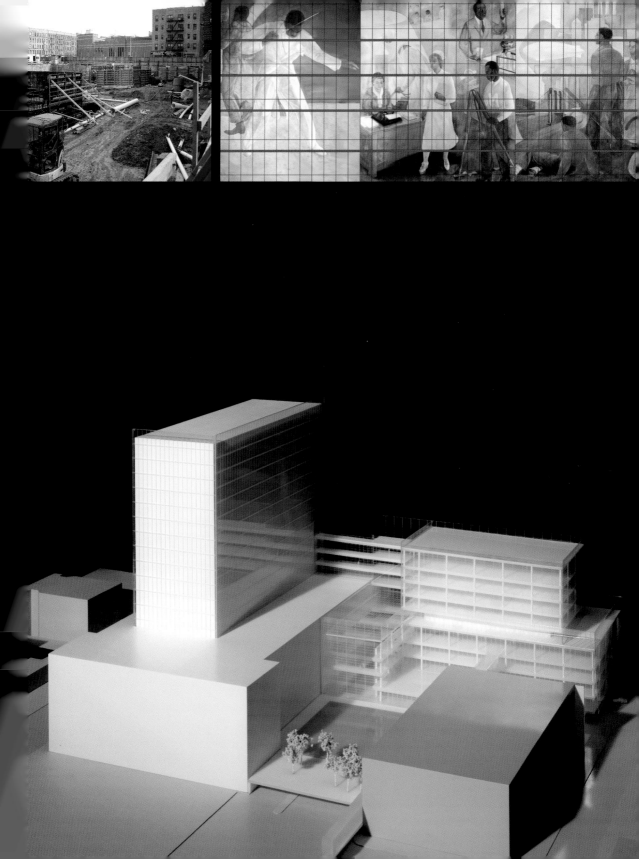

MICHAEL DOLINSKI (LEFT AND RIGHT)

Elisabetta Terragni

Kindergarten and
Elementary School
Altavilla Vicentina, Italy

description In addition to the kindergarten and elementary school, the building accommodates a gymnasium, Mensa, and community auditorium. Classrooms are grouped together in the south and north of the building, its ample vestibule providing an elevated play and study area over a subterranean theater. Classrooms have individual patios shielded by movable sunscreens. And in combination with patios and corridors form an enticing maze containing bathrooms, storage, and recreation areas. ● The concept of the building resides in an extended single-story structure. Three distinct entrances lead to the classrooms of the kindergarten and elementary school, as well as to a sunken auditorium.

PHOTOS: ELISABETTA TERRAGNI (EXCEPT WHERE NOTED)

Albert Vecerka

Untitled

Description: In the late 1990s I started photographing Harlem, and in fall of 2000 I began work on a series of photographs of entire blocks as another way to document the neighborhood. After I first photographed this block, it quickly started to change, which attracted me. In the beginning it was the billboards that were changing but soon buildings started to disappear and eventually the large building on the corner of Lenox Avenue and 125th Street was demolished, leaving the entire length of the block empty. The incomplete physical transformation is symbolic and poses questions of sustainability, morality, and social justice.

IMPOSSIBLE
WORD THROW
SMALL MEN
EASIER TO LIVE
THEY'VE BEE
TO EXPLORE
THEY HAVE
IMPOSSIBLE
IT'S AN OPINIC
IS NOT A DEC
A DARE. IM
POTENTIAL.
IS TEMPORAR
IMPOSSIBLE
FOREVER SPO
FOREVER SPORT
adidas
DON'T BLOCK THE BOX
BETTER WAY
SHOE REPAIR
Stylish Men's Sho
Men's Walker
HATS & ACCESSORIES
Subway
MOVED TO 58 W 125ST
Cashed

PHOTOS: ALBERT VECERKA / ESTO

Christian Volkmann

Nine Square House
Germany

description Planned for a work-at-home couple with their own small marketing firm, this house on the edge of a farming town had to fulfill the client's request for a short construction time and maximum spatial flexibility, and take full advantage of Germany's extensive 'green building subsidies. • The clients wanted the house's image to correspond to the local barn and farmhouse-dotted landscape. At the same time, they had always been fascinated by open loft-like spaces. • The house is conceived as a full timbered, prefabricated structure, wrapped in a 14" insulated shell. The structural concept offers quick construction and 'flowing space' which can be subdivided as needed.

1 FASSADE: WESTANSICHT
A0.7 MASZSTAB: 1:75

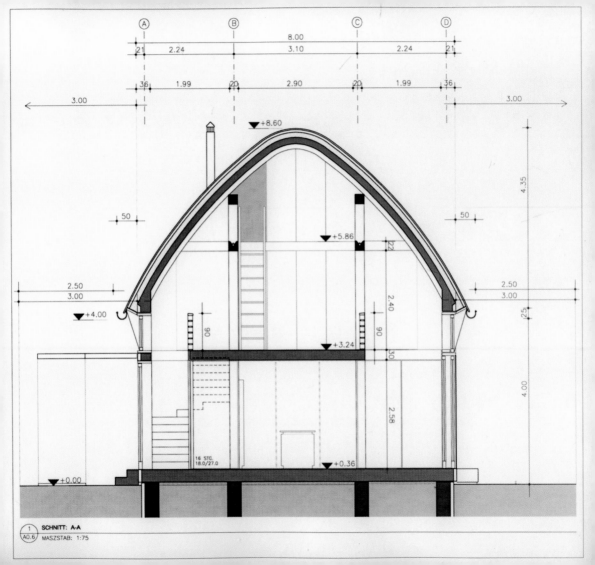

SCHNITT: A-A
MASZSTAB: 1:75

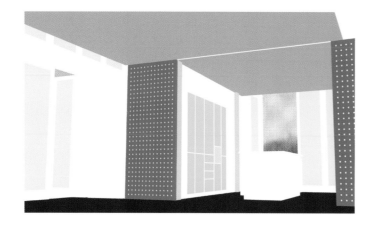

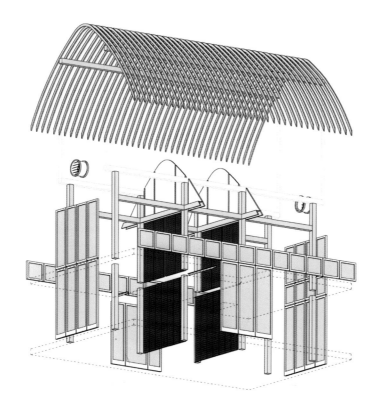

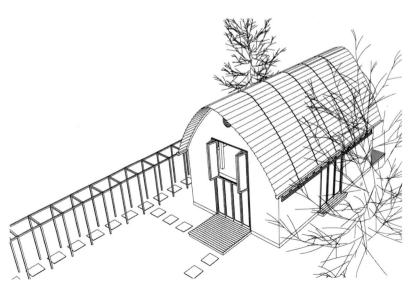

Lee Weintraub

Erie Basin Park
Red Hook, Brooklyn,
New York

description I first came to Red Hook in 1987 and led a storefront community design process that resulted in the construction of the Coffey Street Pier and the development of Valentino Park. In 2002 I returned to Red Hook, an incredibly compelling place filled with memories of the waterfront as a place of commerce and production. Invited by the Ikea Corporation to design a new public waterfront park, Erie Basin Park comprises approximately a mile of green park, esplanade and plaza spaces. Incorporated into the fabric of the park are remains of the site's former occupant, the New York Ship Yard. Four inactive cranes have been stabilized and serve as heroic markers and powerful reminders.

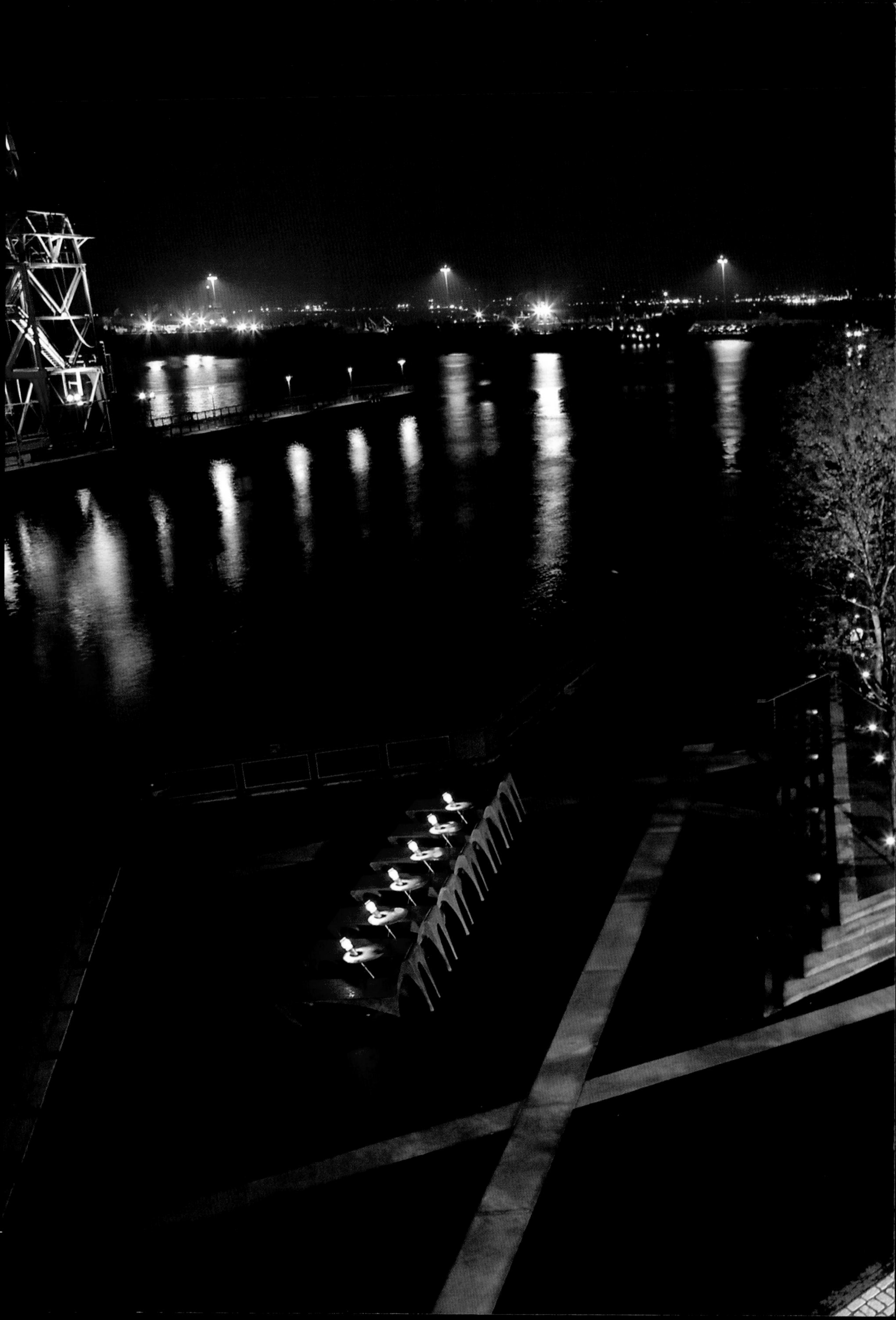

June Williamson

Retrofitting Suburbia: Urban Design Solutions for Redesigning Suburbs
John Wiley & Sons, 2009.

description Co-author Ellen Dunham-Jones and I researched eighty retrofit projects, including numerous examples of aging, stand-alone shopping malls and office parks that have been replaced with multi-block, mixed-use town centers with public squares and greens.

1-4, From Dead Mall to Green Downtown: Belmar, Lakewood, CO
5. Edge City Infill: Downtown Kendall/Dadeland, Miami-Dade County, FL
6. Infilling an Office Park: University Town Center, Prince George's County, MD
7. From Shopping Center to Walkable Village: Mashpee Commons, Mashpee, MA

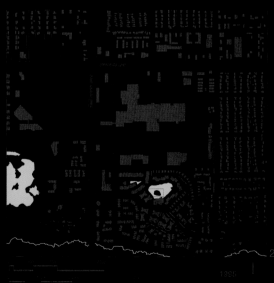

alameda ave.

wadsworth blvd.

w. alaska dr.

s. teller st.

w. virginia ave.

0   500'   1000'   2000'

2015

0   1/8 mi   1/4 mi   1/2 mi

3

1975

500' 1000' 2000'
1/8 mi 1/4 mi 1/2 mi

1995

2015

4

1970

500' 1000' 2000'
1/8 mi 1/4 mi 1/2 mi

1995

2020

5

1940

500' 1000' 2000'
1/8 mi 1/4 mi 1/2 mi

1980

2020

6

1985

500' 1000' 2000'
1/8 mi 1/4 mi 1/2 mi

2005

2025

7

Ap
pen
dix

Faculty & Staff

THE CITY UNIVERSITY OF NEW YORK ADMINISTRATION

Matthew Goldstein
Chancellor

THE CITY COLLEGE OF NEW YORK CUNY ADMINISTRATION

Gregory H. Williams
President

Zeev Dagan
Provost

THE CITY COLLEGE OF NEW YORK BERNARD AND ANNE SPITZER SCHOOL OF ARCHITECTURE

George Ranalli
Dean

Peter Gisolfi
Professor
Chair

Gordon Gebert
Professor
Deputy Chair

Michael Sorkin
Distinguished Professor
Director, Master of Urban
Design Program

Achva Benzinberg Stein
Professor
Director, Master of
Landscape Architecture
Program

Bradley Horn
Assistant Professor
Director, Master of
Architecture Program

Vanessa Alicea
Adjunct Lecturer

Jacob Alspector
Associate Professor

Nandini Bagchee
Adjunct Assistant
Professor

Carmi Bee
Professor Emeritus

Horst Berger
Professor Emeritus

Maria Berman
Adjunct Lecturer

William Bobenhausen
Adjunct Professor

Hillary Brown
Professor

Lance Jay Brown
Professor

Sara Caples
Visiting Professor

Mi-Tsung Chang
Assistant Professor

Timothy Matthew Collins
Adjunct Assistant
Professor

Joan Copjec
Adjunct Professor

Johanna Dickson
Adjunct Lecturer

Antonio Di Oronzo
Adjunct Assistant
Professor

Jeremy Edmiston
Associate Professor

Alan Feigenberg
Professor

Alberto Foyo
Adjunct Professor

Antonio Furgiuele
Adjunct Lecturer

Marta Gutman
Associate Professor

Athanasios Haritos
Adjunct Lecturer

Daniel Hauben
Adjunct Lecturer

Ghislaine Hermanuz
Professor

Ali Höcek
Adjunct Associate
Professor

Denise Hoffman Brandt
Associate Professor

Leonard Hopper
Adjunct Assistant
Professor

Lewis Iglehart
Adjunct Professor

Marcha Johnson
Adjunct Professor

David Judelson
Adjunct Assistant
Professor

Vanessa Keith
Adjunct Assistant
Professor

Fran Leadon
Assistant Professor

Peter Lippman
Adjunct Lecturer

Fabian Llonch
Associate Professor

Peter Lynch
Adjunct Professor

Hanque Macari
Professor

W. Garrison McNeil
Professor Emeritus

Donald Mongitore
Adjunct Professor

Jose Oubrerie
Visiting Professor

Irma Ostroff
Adjunct Professor

Dominick Pilla
Adjunct Professor

Ivan Rosa
Adjunct Associate
Professor

Julio Salcedo-Fernandez
Associate Professor

Morris Silberberg
Adjunct Professor

Malka Simon
Adjunct Lecturer

Neal Spanier
Adjunct Professor

Elisabetta Terragni
Associate Professor

Robert Twombly
Adjunct Professor

Albert Vecerka
Adjunct Associate
Professor

Christian Volkmann
Associate Professor

Anthony Walmsley
Adjunct Professor

Lee Weintraub
Associate Professor

June Williamson
Associate Professor

Suzan Wines
Adjunct Associate
Professor

Ching-Jung Chen
Art and Architecture Slide
Librarian

Carolina Colon
Assistant to the
Chairperson

Judy Connorton
Director
School of Architecture
Library

Junko Fujimoto
Assistant Slide Librarian

Camille Hall
Director of Finance
and Administration

Ghislaine Hermanuz
Director of Advising

Arnaldo Melendez
Undergraduate Advisor

Sara Morales
Graduate Advisor

Nilda Sanchez
Architecture Library Assist

Kathleen Sheridan
Executive Assistant
to the Dean

Emily Ferrari
School of Architecture Office
Assistant

Rosa Santos
Slide Library Assistant

Faculty Bios

GEORGE RANALLI, Dean George Ranalli has been Dean of the Bernard and Anne Spitzer School of Architecture at City College since 1999. He was born and raised in New York City. He received his Bachelor of Architecture from Pratt Institute in 1972 and Master of Architecture from the Graduate School of Design at Harvard University in 1974. From 1976-1999 he was Professor of Architecture at Yale University, and in 1988–1989 he was the William Henry Bishop Chaired Professor in Architectural Design. Mr. Ranalli recently completed his fourth monograph, Saratoga, devoted to his Saratoga Avenue Community Center for the New York City Housing Authority. That project has been widely praised, notably in a May 13, 2009 article by Ada Louis Huxtable in The Wall Street Journal. His architectural and design work has been published internationally in numerous journals including Domus, A+U, Progressive Architecture, L'Architettura, G.A. Houses, Architectural Digest, Architecture D'Aujourd'hui, Architectural Design, and Lotus. His work has been exhibited at the Cooper–Hewitt Museum, Sperone–Westwater Gallery, the Museum of Contemporary Art in Chicago, the Museum of Finnish Architecture, Centre Pompidou in France, Deutsches Architekturmuseum in Frankfurt, the XVII Triennale Di Milano in Italy, and a one-man exhibit at Artists Space Gallery in New York in 1998. He designed the exhibition Frank Lloyd Wright: Designs for an American Landscape, 1922-1932 for the Whitney Museum of Art in 1997, and designed the installation for the exhibition of work of Carlo Scarpa, in 1999 at the Canadian Centre for Architecture Montreal, Canada.

PETER GISOLFI, Chair Peter Gisolfi is a Professor and Chairman of the School. He is an architect, landscape architect, and teacher whose work reconciles the influences of context and program. His concern for the relationship of architecture to its setting translates into graceful connections between buildings and landscapes. His analytical approach to design was inspired by undergraduate studies in music theory and composition at Yale, and graduate training in architecture and landscape architecture at the University of Pennsylvania. Mr. Gisolfi was previously an Adjunct Associate Professor of Architecture at Columbia University for twelve years. The work of Peter Gisolfi Associates receives many design awards, and is featured in the press and numerous books.

JACOB ALSPECTOR, Associate Professor Jacob Alspector currently teaches 5th Year Thesis and Iconic Building Tectonics. Prior to joining the faculty in 2003, he held the Fitz-Gibbon Visiting Professor Chair at Carnegie Mellon. A product of the New York City public schools, he attended Brooklyn Tech, Cooper Union, and the Institute for Architecture and Urban Studies. He served as a Trustee of Cooper, received their President's Citation, and was President of their Alumni Association. As principal of Alspector Architecture his recent built work includes the Utah Valley University Library, the Grace Church School Gymnasium and renovations to NYU's Bobst Library. Until 2002, Alspector, as Associate Partner at Gwathmey Siegel, was responsible for many award-winning designs.

NANDINI BAGCHEE, Adjunct Assistant Professor Nandini Bagchee is an architect based in New York City. She grew up in India and moved to New York to study architecture at Cooper Union. In 2005 she began an independent architectural practice based in Brooklyn. Her practice is currently engaged in designing and coordinating residential and institutional projects in New York and its environs. The work produced in her studio responds to the conditions of the city and explores the changing narratives that create a need for architecture. She has studied Islamic art, urbanism, and landscape, and brings an understanding of culture, nature and history to her architectural work. In 2003 her entry for the Great Egyptian Museum in Cairo was published in a catalog by the museum to honor the winning entries. She was the recipient of the Agha Khan study grant for Islamic Architecture (1998-2000).

ACHVA BENZINBERG STEIN, Professor Achva Benzinberg Stein is a professor and practicing professional who has taught and worked in the US, Europe, Israel, India, and China. Her projects with neighborhood groups, public agencies, and non-profit organizations concentrate on meeting social needs while seeking to heal the damage of poorly managed urban development. Her landscape designs, which have won numerous awards from the American Society of Landscape Architects has included designs for school grounds, large-scale housing projects, parks, playgrounds, hotels, community gardens and private residences. She has won numerous awards, including the 1994 Chrysler Award for Innovation in Design, and has twice been the recipient of Fulbright grants.

MARIA BERMAN, Adjunct Lecturer Maria Berman is principal along with Brad Horn of Berman Horn Studio whose work has been featured in publications such as Architectural Record, The Architect's Newspaper, and most recently in the book Taschen's New York (2009). She writes for several art publications and has exhibited work in New York City galleries. She has also served on the faculty at Parsons School of Design and Pratt Institute. Before entering the field of design she practiced as an art conservator at major New York City museums including the Museum of Modern Art and the Cooper-Hewitt National Design Museum. She holds undergraduate and masters degrees from the University of Chicago and NYU Institute of Fine Arts and received her Master of Architecture degree from Columbia University.

LANCE JAY BROWN, Professor Lance Jay Brown, FAIA, is an architect, urban designer, author and ACSA Distinguished Professor, where he was two-term Chair and Director. He is a Fellow of the Institute for Urban Design and board member of the AIA/NYC. He was 2005 Chair of the AIA national Regional and Urban Design Committee. From 1979 to 1983 he served as Special Consultant to the Design Arts Program of the National Endowment for the Arts. In 2007 he was awarded the AIA / ACSA Topaz Medallion, the highest honor given to an architectural educator in the United States. He recently co-authored Urban Design For An Urban Century (Wiley, January 2009). He was educated at the Cooper Union and holds two masters degrees from the GSD at Harvard.

MI-TSUNG CHANG, Assistant Professor Mi-Tsung Chang received his Bachelor of Architecture degree in 1989 and Master of Architecture degree from Pratt Institute in 1991. He received his Ph. D. in 1996 from the Union Institute in Ohio and began his teaching career at CCNY in 1999 and has served as director of Computer Services & Digital Media Labs from 1999 to present. During his tenure as director he successfully modernized and expanded the lab and enhanced its research capacity. His expertise includes architecture technology, tall building design, intelligent building design, and digital architecture. He teaches courses in technology, theory, and CAD. He is the principal of Hypnos Design. He currently lives in New York City.

TIMOTHY COLLINS, Adjunct Assistant Professor Timothy Matthew Collins was born in Buffalo, New York and currently lives and works in New York City. After receiving a B.Arch from the Cooper Union for the Advancement of Science and Art in 2003, he spent a year studying in Firenze, Italia for an M.Arch degree from Syracuse University. Since then, Mr. Collins has worked as a designer for the international architectural firm RMJM (formerly Hillier) and has taught architecture, drawing, and visualization at multiple universities. His personal work, which revolves around issues of collage, history, and landscape, has been featured in museum collections as well as multiple exhibitions both in the United States and abroad.

ANTONIO DI ORONZO, Adjunct Assistant Professor Antonio Di Oronzo came to New York from Rome, Italy in 1997 and has been practicing architecture and interior design for fifteen years. He is a Doctor in Architecture from the University of Rome "La Sapienza", and has a Masters in Urban Planning from CCNY. He also holds a post-graduate degree in Construction Management from the Italian Army Academy. He has worked at internationally recognized firms such as Eisenman Architects, Robert Siegel Architects, and Gruzen Samton. In 2004, he founded the award-winning firm bluarch architecture + interiors + urban planning. The firm has been recognized for its work in publications and exhibitions at MoMA, The Van Alen Institute, and Centro Arquitectum in Caracas, Venezuela.

JEREMY EDMISTON, Associate Professor Jeremy Edmiston is the principal at SYSTEMarchitects. He has been practicing, teaching and researching architecture in New York City for 18 years. His practice seeks to re-evaluate the relationship between the built and natural environment. Originally from Sydney, Australia, he moved to the U.S. when he won Fulbright, Harkness and Byera Hadley scholarships. Other honors include a Lindbergh Fellowship and a Department of Energy's Center of Excellence Fellowship. In 2008, MoMA exhibited the Burst008 house he designed with Douglas Gauthier. Recently the work has been published in Bauwelt, Domus, the New York Times, The New York Review of Books, Le Figaro, The Financial Times, The Washington Post, and the Huffington Post.

ALAN FEIGENBERG, Professor Alan Feigenberg has previously focused his architecture on buildings of public service, day care centers, health clinics and community service centers. He was a founder and director of education for the salvadori center which works with teachers and students in New York City facilitating math and science learning through urban explorations. He has been a co-investigator for over 45 funding grants that seek to use our built urban environments as a source for integrated learning. His unique photography has been exhibited in shows and galleries for the last twenty years.

ALBERTO FOYO, Adjunct Professor Born in Madrid, Spain, Alberto Foyo is the principal of Alberto Foyo Architect, PC. He studied architecture at the Polithecnical School of Architecture in Madrid, Spain and at the University of Oregon in the USA. Upon completion of his studies he worked for five years in New York as chief designer of a large architectural firm in Manhattan. In 1990 he moved to Vienna to collaborate with the Austrian architect Dr. Roland Rainer in the development of residential settlements based on the principles of low rise- high density. In 1992 he returned to New York and opened his independent practice. Since then he has also sustained involvement with the discipline of architecture as international guest critic, lecturer, and professor. His office is involved in projects that include urban planning, architecture, landscape architecture, and interior design in the United States, Spain, Ukraine, and most recently in the Amazon basin in Brazil where his firm is designing a permaculture and agro forestry research center in collaboration with the local Munduruku tribe.

ATHANASIOS HARITOS, Adjunct Lecturer Athanasios Haritos was born in Melbourne, Australia, and studied Architecture at CCNY and at Columbia University. His work has been recognized and published internationally in many notable architectural journals and books including, Architectural Record, Design + Art in Greece, and The Phaidon Atlas of Contemporary World Architecture. He is a registered architect with The Technical Chamber of Greece and is presently teaching and working in New York.

GHISLAINE HERMANUZ, Professor Ghislaine Hermanuz is an architect and urban designer. Her professional work in the United States has concentrated on community design, starting with the Architects' Renewal Committee in Harlem, the first design center created by black architects, later as the director of the City College Architectural Center and now as a consultant to the Urban Technical Assistance Project/ Columbia University. Her work consists of neighborhood development plans and visualization of physical development concepts and proposals. She regularly contributes to UN- sponsored efforts to advance shelter provision, with a focus on the needs and perspectives of women. Recently her research has dealt with the impact of the Environmental Justice movement on the transformation of inner city neighborhoods.

ALI C. HÖCEK, Adjunct Associate Professor Ali Höcek has been practicing independently since 1989, and his architectural firm has a diverse and unique project base, ranging from an addition to the Avari Hotel in Lahore, Pakistan (a Brutalist work designed by members of Team X) to museum and exhibition installations for clients such as the Guggenheim and the Museum of the Moving Image. More recently, he formed Think OffSite, which is primarily engaged in the delivery of prefabricated housing and academic buildings. He has been publicly recognized by such institutions as the NYC Landmarks Preservation Commission and the AIA-NY Chapter. He is licensed in New York and Rhode Island. He studied at the Rhode Island School of Design and at the Architectural Association in London, and holds an M.A. in Architecture from Syracuse University in Florence, Italy.

DENISE HOFFMAN BRANDT, Associate Professor Denise Hoffman Brandt is a professor of Landscape Architecture at CCNY, and principal of Hoffman Brandt Landscape Design in New York City. Her work focuses on landscape as infrastructure; the social, cultural and environmental systems that sustain urban life and generate urban form. She received a New York Prize Fellowship from the Van Alen Institute to investigate the physical, economic, and policy potential to catalyze urban carbon sequestration reservoirs, or sinks, in New York City. Her project for revitalizing a refugee encampment through new energy and waste infrastructure in Kenya was featured in a workshop on the right to landscape and received an honorable mention in the Architectural Association's Environmental Tectonics Competition.

BRADLEY HORN, Assistant Professor Director, Master of Architecture Program Brad Horn is principal along with Maria Berman of Berman Horn Studio, whose work has been featured in publications such as Architectural Record, The Architect's Newspaper, and most recently in the book Taschen's New York (2009). His writing has been published in Frieze Magazine, Journal of Architecture and Computation Culture, and The Architect's Newspaper as well as in the books Autogenic Structures from Taylor and Francis Press and Ineffable, forthcoming from Oscar Riera Ojeda Publishers (2009). Horn has taught design at The Cooper Union, Harvard University Graduate School of Design, Pratt Institute, and Columbia University.

LEWIS IGLEHART, Adjunct Professor Lewis Iglehart is an architect who lives and works in Brooklyn, New York. A graduate of Pratt Institute and a member of the American Institute of Architects, his practice provides illustration and design consultation services to architects and developers in this country and abroad. He teaches the elective course Advanced Presentation Techniques at CCNY.

DAVID JUDELSON, Adjunct Assistant Professor David Judelson has designed architectural projects that range from a computer center for the Aero Engine Division of Rolls Royce and a new town on the eastern edge of London to sets and props for theater and dance performances. He has designed and developed a number of live/work cooperatives and condominiums for artists in Boston and New York. He is an award-winning sculptor, with eight solo exhibitions and numerous group shows as well as public and private commissions. And he has also taught architectural design at MIT and at Northeastern University. He is currently working on a book on creativity, Freedom to Create.

FRAN LEADON, Assistant Professor Fran Leadon has been a full-time member of the faculty at CCNY since 2000, and the first-year studio coordinator since 2004. He is a registered architect in New York State and is co-author, with Norval White, of the upcoming AIA Guide to New York City, Fifth Edition (Oxford University Press, 2010). He writes regularly for Oculus and e-Oculus. He received a Bachelor of Design (in Architecture) degree from the University of Florida in 1991 and a Master of Architecture degree from Yale University in 1994. He is a member of the American Institute of Architects and serves on the Advisory Board at the Queens Museum of Art. He received the Faculty of the Year award from the student organization CCAP in 2005. He was born and raised in Gainesville, Florida.

PETER LYNCH, Adjunct Professor Peter Lynch opened his architecture practice in New York City in 1991. He collaborates with Ahlaiya Yung in the international studio Metasus and with Gustavo Crembil in the studio THEM. He co-directs Building Culture, an international non-profit dedicated to advancing sustainable design. He served as Architect-in-Residence and head of graduate architecture department at Cranbrook Academy of Art from 1996 to 2005. He is External Examiner, Dalhousie University Faculty of Architecture, Halifax, from 2003 to the present. He was named an "Emerging Voice in Architecture" by the Architectural League of New York in 2003. He won a Progressive Architecture Award in 2005 and the Rome Prize in 2004-05.

IVAN ROSA, Adjunct Associate Professor Ivan Rosa has practiced architecture, landscape architecture and urban design, including projects for Octagon Park on Roosevelt Island and the 125th Metro-North Station rehabilitation with Weintraub & di Domenico. With Hillier he designed the Valle Arriba Athletic Club in Venezuela and a 550 acre masterplan for the University at Albany. Currently, Mr. Rosa is a Studio Director with TPG Architecture where he is working on exhibition space for 'Terra Cotta Warriors' and a masterplan for the National Geographic Society, as well as the renovation of the United Way of America Headquarters, both in the Washington, DC area. He is a graduate of CCNY where he received a B.S. in Landscape Architecture and a Bachelor of Architecture. He also holds a M.S. in Architecture & Urban Design from Columbia University.

JULIO SALCEDO-FERNANDEZ, Associate Professor Julio Salcedo-Fernandez was born in Madrid, Spain. He studied architecture at Rice University and Harvard's Graduate School of Design. He previously taught at Harvard, Syracuse University, the University of Pennsylvania, and Cornell University prior to joining the faculty at CCNY. His areas of research and teaching deal with the design continuum of generic and specific modes as they apply to several categories, including relationships between architecture, landscape, urbanism, housing and tectonics. He has been widely published and has contributed to various periodicals including Pasajes, Arquitectura and Praxis. He formed the practice Scalar Architecture in 2001.

MICHAEL SORKIN, Distinguished Professor. Director, Master of Urban Design Program Michael Sorkin is the principal of Michael Sorkin Studio in New York City, a design practice devoted to both practical and theoretical projects at all scales with a special interest in the city and in green architecture. Recent projects include planning and design for a highly sustainable 5000-unit community in Penang, Malaysia, master planning for the Zha Bei district in Shanghai, the design of a town of 40,000 on the Black Sea in Turkey, a hotel in Tianjin, China, planning for a Palestinian capital in East Jerusalem, campus planning at the University of Chicago and Hebei University, studies of the Manhattan and Brooklyn waterfronts, and housing in Far Rockaway, Vienna, and Miami.

ELISABETTA TERRAGNI, Associate Professor After graduating from Milan Polytechnic, Elisabetta Terragni served on the faculty at the Federal Institute of Technology (ETH) and established her own office in Como, Italy. She has been Associate Professor at CCNY since Fall, 2008. She won a competition in 2003 for a major public school building in the town of Altavilla Vicentina (Vicenza). The project includes an indoor sports court, as well as a small theater for the community. A special solution for the roof was evolved in collaboration with the Swiss engineer Juerg Conzett (Chur), allowing for a tensioned roof slab of over 250 feet in length. With its surface of 32,000 square feet, the building embraces several patios and additional areas for recreational and pedagogical use.

ALBERT VECERKA, Adjunct Associate Professor A native of the former Yugoslavia, Albert Vecerka moved to New York in 1992. He received a BS in Architecture from City College in 1997. The following year he began to concentrate on photography, working as an assistant and shooting his own assignments as well. In 2002 he began his affiliation with Esto, an agency formed by Ezra Stoller that specializes in architectural photography. Since then he has worked on a variety of projects for large and small clients, photographing the IAC Building, the Visitors Center for NYC&CO, the Clinton Library, the Harlem Children's Zone, and the Walker Art Center, to name a few. He taught photography and woodworking at Parsons School of Design; currently he teaches architectural photography at City College and as a continuing education course at The Cooper Union.

CHRISTIAN VOLKMANN, Associate Professor Christian Volkmann has been a full-time faculty member at CCNY since 2008, and part-time faculty beginning in 2005. His teaching has focused on seminars and studios that integrate technical and environmental topics into the design process. He was Adjunct Professor of Architecture at the Rhode Island School of Design from 2001 to 2008. He is a registered architect in New York State, and practices in New York City as principal of aardvarchitecture. He studied in Berlin and Zurich, receiving a Master of Architecture degree from the Swiss Federal Polytechnic University Zurich in 1992. He has worked, among others, for J.P. Kleihues (Berlin), Mario Campi (Lugano) and Annabelle Selldorf (New York). He was born and raised in Hildesheim, Germany.

JUNE WILLIAMSON, Associate Professor June Williamson is an urban designer and registered architect with over 16 years of experience in design and teaching throughout the United States. June is co-author, with Ellen Dunham-Jones, of Retrofitting Suburbia: Urban Design Solutions for Redesigning Suburbs (John Wiley & Sons, 2009), a case study book of over 80 examples of the remarkable changes that are occurring as dead malls, empty big box stores, low density office parks, aging apartment complexes, and other single-use developments are being remade to meet new economic, demographic, and environmental challenges. June is an active Fellow of the Institute for Urban Design. She has degrees from Yale, MIT and CCNY.

Oscar Riera Ojeda **Publishers**
A division of Novus Creative Group

www.oscarrieraojeda.com

USA: 143 South Second Street, Suite 208,
Philadelphia, PA 19106-3073 Telephone: 1-215-238-1333

Singapore: 80 Raffles Place, UOB Plaza 1, Level 36-01,
Singapore 048624 Telephone: 65-6248-4596

Argentina: Avenida Santa Fe 2161 piso 11 C1425ELM,
Buenos Aires Telephone: 54-11-4821-9195

info@oscarrieraojeda.com

Copyright © 2009 by Oscar Riera Ojeda Publishers

ISBN 978-981-08-3966-6

Publication Credits
Editor: Fran Leadon
Graphic Design: Oscar Riera Ojeda, Esteban Martucci, Leo Malinow, and Flor Saltamartini
Copy Editing: Azliana Abdullah
Project Assistance: Bruno Serrien
Production: Oscar Riera Ojeda and Bruno Serrien
Color Separation and Printing: Novus Books Singapore
Covers: 360 gsm coated two side Artcard
Text Paper: 170 gsm Arrow matt art paper from Sweden; an off-line gloss spot varnish was applied
to all photographs.

Distribution: Novus Creative Group